Servant Governing

THE FOUR CORNERSTONES OF THE FRAMEWORK FOR EXCELLENCE IN GOVERNMENT

by Ed Dean

Copyright © 2013 Ed Dean
All rights reserved.

ISBN: 1492210242
ISBN 13: 9781492210245

Letter from John Pieno, Jr.

I applaud your description of "Servant Governing." It should be a clear requirement for all public officials to read.

The term, public servant, is much used in local, state, and federal government to describe the workforce that has been employed to serve the needs of citizens. Not a new term, but one that is the most applicable description is "Servant Governing." You clearly and succinctly describe what that should mean and what should be expected of all of us who truly want to serve the public.

I commend your effort and would make this book required reading for all "public servants."

John Pieno, Jr., President
Florida Sterling Council

ACKNOWLEDGEMENTS

I want to thank my family, especially my wife, Sarah, and my friends for being so supportive of me during my fourteen plus years of public service as sheriff of Marion County, Florida.

I also want to thank the citizens of Marion County for giving me the opportunity to serve them as their sheriff which has allowed me over the years to put into practice the Four Cornerstones of Servant Governing.

I owe a debt of gratitude to all the dedicated men and women of the Marion County Sheriff's Office who willingly embraced the culture of Servant Governing and who demonstrated role model status through their achievements and performance which culminated in the Marion County Sheriff's Office receiving the Florida Governor's Sterling Award.

I appreciate the kind letter of endorsement from Mr. John Pieno, president of the Florida Sterling Council. Congratulations to the council for its fine work.

Ms. Janie Krohne and Ms. Terri Judy are thanked for their outstanding assistance and their patience with me in putting this book together.

"Thank you" to several of my close friends who took the time to review a preliminary draft of this work and offer good suggestions for its improvement. Lastly, I want to thank Ms. Robin Swift of the Servant Leadership Institute for her helpful suggestions regarding the publication of this book.

DEDICATION

This book is dedicated to the men and women who work in federal, state and local government who are committed to the belief that citizens are deserving of the highest level of performance excellence achievable in their government.

TABLE OF CONTENTS

Endorsement iii

Acknowledgments v

Dedication vii

Table of Contents ix

Prologue xi

Chapter One: Introduction 1

Chapter Two: Servant Governing Defined 11

Chapter Three: The People Cornerstone 17

Chapter Four: The Principles Cornerstone 31

Chapter Five: The Priorities Cornerstone 41

Chapter Six: The Performance Cornerstone 55

Chapter Seven: The Sailboat Analogy 63

Chapter Eight: Conclusion 71

Epilogue 77

Bibliography 83

Appendices

Florida Sterling Criteria for Performance
     Excellence (2013) 87

Marion County Sheriff's Office Sustained Excellence
     Award Application (2011) 113

Library of Suggested Reading 165

Servant Leadership: Accepting and Maintaining the
     Call of Service 169

PROLOGUE

Over the years of my experience in publicly traded and privately held business organizations, coupled with my fourteen years of experience as an elected Sheriff in charge of a large Florida Sheriff's office, I have observed different organizational cultures and how they affect the employees who work in those cultures. As an employee, I have seen many leaders in operation from the entrepreneurial leader who chooses to be involved in every decision to leaders who are rarely involved with the workforce, except regarding matters involving corporate policy and profits. I have also seen organizations face seemingly impossible odds against their survival, but despite those odds, they did survive and go on to great accomplishments. On the other hand, I have witnessed previously well-run organizations ultimately fail because no one seemed to care anymore and corporate greed prevailed.

Like most people, I have experienced extremely kind treatment as an employee and at other times I have experienced cavalier treatment by supervisors. I have experienced generosity within the workplace, and I have experienced austerity. I have known the pleasure of being complimented for a job well done and I have been the recipient of unappreciative attitudes for my accomplishments. I know first-hand how rewarding it feels to participate in decision-making as an employee and I also know the frustration which exists when good ideas are ignored and unwelcomed in an organization.

The aforementioned laundry list of experiences I have had over the years has helped me to better understand what motivates people to do a good job; what gives them security in their employment; and what kind of culture brings out the best performance in employees. I have learned how an organization can best harness the creative energy of its workforce; and how organizations can translate that energy into problem solving and high performance results.

In government service, I have witnessed first-hand how the culture within an organization can make all the difference in determining whether the public's interest is stagnated by mediocre performance, or whether the public's interest and the public good are being ratcheted up through high performance results. I have also witnessed the effects of multi-year downward economic trends and the accompanying loss of revenue in both business and in government. I have experienced the necessity of shrinking private and public organizations to meet reduced projected revenues without adversely affecting performance.

I have seen how adherence to the core values of an organization helped to transform the organization. I have also witnessed major core values violations which have occurred in an organization and how the organization dealt with those violations. I have experienced the exhilaration of strategic objective accomplishments within a well-planned organization, and I have seen how an organization can flounder without strategic thinking.

What I have concluded from my own experiences is that the only way difficult challenges can be met and problems overcome in either private or public organizations, over the long haul, is through creative thinking by the people in the organization. I believe the level of creative thinking within an organization is dependent upon the kind of leadership culture that exists in the organization. Without a culture that fosters creativity, an organization which is facing threatening challenges will not succeed. In such cases, businesses will fail.

In government, because government cannot really fail, the government organization which lacks creative thinking becomes mired in average or poor performance.

In regard to leadership, I have seen a variety of leadership styles in organizations ranging from egocentric, personality driven leaders who shoot first and ask questions later, to bureaucratic leaders who do not have the will power to make necessary changes in time to avert impending calamities.

Within the full range of leadership styles, there is one leadership philosophy and practice which has stood out in my mind. It is leading with a servant's heart. People are attracted to leaders with a servant's heart. People believe that leaders with a servant's heart genuinely care. I am not referring to leaders who are timid or "weak-kneed." I am referring to leaders who care enough to do things the right way and invest the time and energy needed to serve others.

Now we come to the reason for writing this book. I believe a change in governing culture is vitally necessary in order to transform the manner in which many government organizations operate. As stated previously, businesses either change the way they do business or they go out of business when current challenges are not being met. However, government is perpetual which makes it more difficult to change in order to attain performance excellence as compared to its business counterparts.

The main premise of this book is that government organizations can achieve performance excellence through the adoption of the proven principles set forth in this writing. It is time to adopt and implement a new leadership and management framework within the government which serves us all.

The adoption and implementation of the Servant Governing Framework will ultimately lead to higher performance results for the government organization. Servant Governing stimulates creativity, mission focus, performance results and job satisfaction within organizations. Servant Governing is premised upon the belief that achievement of performance excellence in service to the citizens served by the government organization is not only desirable, but necessary.

This book is not intended to be a detailed treatment of every leadership and management concept which is discussed herein. Rather, the book is intended to be an overview examination of the interdependent nature of the various leadership and management elements of Servant Governing with an eye toward giving the reader insight as to how a government organizational culture can be transformed; and, what is needed to transform it. More detailed information regarding the elements which comprise Servant Governing can be found in the resource material set forth in the Appendices at the end of the book.

Practical pointers are included at the end of several chapters of the book to aid the implementation of the Servant Governing Framework.

The opinions and recommendations contained in this book are solely mine. Reference to any person or organization is not to be construed as an endorsement of my opinion or recommendations.

Thank you.

Ed Dean
Copyrighted – 2013

> "A small group of thoughtful people can change the world.
> Indeed, it's the only thing that has."
>
> — MARGARET MEAD

Chapter One

Introduction

- ❦ Question "Zero"
- ❦ Excellence vs. Mediocrity
- ❦ Governing Smarter

Question "Zero"

At the Harvard University John F. Kennedy School of Government, students are taught to ask Question "Zero" when considering a new policy, issue or initiative. Question "Zero" is, "What are we trying to accomplish?"

What, then, is the author of a book entitled *Servant Governing* trying to accomplish? The simple answer is that there is a way to achieve excellence in government performance. It is with the utmost humility that this writing will suggest a new governance model which has application to federal, state and local government operations.

Most states and their local government counterparts have governing challenges and need solutions to be found to meet those challenges. The solutions needed to meet persistent government challenges that can be found through a change in the governance culture. A new governance culture is needed in order to harness the creativity needed to meet today's governing challenges and the challenges which will come. This book will offer the suggestion for a new high performance governance culture which can be achieved through Servant Governing.

EXCELLENCE VS. MEDIOCRITY

As the tide of the Great Recession begins to recede, many people in America are hoping a new tide of prosperity will begin to emerge, a strong economy will be created and that it will last a long time. In every state and in every locality of this great nation, people have felt the adverse effects of a poor economy to some degree or another. On the local level, city and county governments have struggled to maintain essential services, while other government organizations have had to cut government services just to survive. State governments, to a varying degree, have had to make difficult choices on what programs need to be reduced or eliminated and which ones will remain intact. Unfortunately, the critical areas of public safety, education, healthcare and children's programs have not been spared the budget knife in many states, or by the federal government.

The process of "weathering the storm" of economic uncertainty and experiencing revenue free-falls have left many leaders in federal, state and local government organizations scratching their heads and wondering how things can be turned around. As the economy improves, the debate continues as to whether more regulation or less regulation is the answer to keeping the economy growing and to achieving full employment.

The United States economy is still the world's largest national economy; and, the United States is one of the world's wealthiest nations with abundant natural resources, including a well-developed infrastructure. The United States also can boast that of the world's 500 largest companies, 132 are headquartered in the United States, twice that of any other country.

America's military is the strongest and best equipped in the world. People all over the world look to America as the defender of freedom and the beacon of opportunity. America is exceptional.

Notwithstanding the economic prowess and military of this great nation and her people, America still faces many challenges on the home front which primarily stem from government's inability to solve long-term systemic problems. For example, the number of children living in poverty has reached record high levels. The United States spends more per capita on healthcare than any other nation, but life expectancy is less than 17 other high-income countries.

(See http://en.wikipedia.org/wiki/International rankings of the United States; http://creativecommons.org)

According to a 2012 New York Times article regarding education rankings, the U.S. ranks 17th in fourth-grade math, 9th in eighth-grade math, 7th in fourth grade science, 10th in eighth-grade science, and 6th in fourth-grade reading as compared to other industrialized nations. (See *U.S. Students Still Lag Globally in Math and Science Tests Show.* By Mokoto Rich, December 11, 2012).

In the area of crime prevention, U.S. ranks 7th in homicides out of 87 countries, 1st in death by violence out of 17 "high income democracies", and 1st in cocaine use. In regard to children's issues, the U.S. ranks 34th out of forty-three developed countries in children's index, 2nd out of thirty-five advanced countries in child poverty, and 178th in child mortality.

(See http://rankingamerica.wordpress.com/how-does-the-united-states-rank-in/)

Despite the tremendous ability of the American people to create business opportunity (number one in new patents), U.S. competitiveness slipped last year from 5th to 7th out of 144 economies according to the World Economic Forum which ranks economics based upon 12 "pillars of competition", including government debt, institutions and infrastructures. (See The Washington Post article dated September 5, 2012, "U.S. Slips in World Economic Forum's Competitiveness Rankings", by Ernie Kolawole)

Based upon the foregoing, it is evident that the private sector is doing its part to strengthen the U.S. economic recovery, but the public sector, which is responsible for addressing many quality of life issues, has not performed as well. Although many government organizations in different states and localities are striving for performance excellence, others have not. Therein lies the problem. All government organizations must contribute to the achievement of overall performance excellence. As a government entity of mediocre performance, America has begun to lag behind other nations in many areas.

Even with all the downsizing, right sizing and emphasis on government efficiency, government organizations still struggle with performance. More and more school districts, city councils, public safety agencies, county commissions and some state and federal organizations are desperately searching for ways to improve the lackluster performance of the past. These government entities and their respective citizens that they serve are collectively weary and frustrated with the repeated, low performance ratings experienced in such key area as job creation, crime prevention, educational achievement and healthcare. These entities of government are looking for answers which will help them break through the barriers to high performance. More money is not the sole answer.

On the other hand, there are government entities on the local, state and federal levels which, unfortunately, are not searching for new answers to old problems. Their leadership seems to be content to continue as they have in the past. After all, keeping a low profile by avoiding conflict and the associated risk of criticism is sometimes more of a priority in some government organizations than achieving excellence. Political survival in government circles is not limited to the elected officials.

Survival paralysis can also affect the whole body politic if leadership is lacking, and if the citizens who are being served do not know what is going on. The latter is the case especially when the media is not exercising its proper role in society as the watch dog of government.

In most states and localities there exists a dedicated and competent work force, both in the private sector and in the public sector. Typically, in government organizations there is not a workforce problem which hinders performance excellence. Rather, mediocre and poor performance in government more often are the result of a leadership problem. The leadership problem is a result of not knowing how performance excellence can be achieved.

If citizens are given a choice between achieving government performance excellence and continuing low government performance, citizens will choose excellence, especially if the cost is the same. Naysayers will quickly point out that citizens today will not approve tax increases and, therefore, change is impossible and low performance is the inevitable result. However, the lack of money is not the main reason for the lack of high performance in government. It is the absence of the governance culture necessary to achieve performance excellence.

Government needs to be effective and efficient. However, government is only truly effective and efficient when government is creative. A creative government culture is able to solve problems. A government culture which is bloated, unnecessarily expensive and bureaucratic lacks the necessary problem-solving creativity just as much as the stripped-down, anemic and unimaginative version. The lack of creativity in government results in missed opportunities for improvement of the public good.

In business and in government, ideas arise from creativity. Opportunity for improvement can then be envisioned through such ideas. Government and businesses must have creativity in order to be successful. The difference between the public sector and the private sector is that in the private sector, if you are not creative, if you do not have ideas, and if you do not seize opportunity when it is presented, you will soon be out of business.

Likewise, in the public sector where creativity does not exist, there will be a lack of ideas. Consequently, without ideas the opportunities to advance the public good remain unseen. As stated previously, however, unlike business, government does not ever "go out of business" and fail. It just continues to operate in a mediocre fashion, not able to solve systemic problems and needless political divisiveness remains. Thus, creative ideas and opportunity, in both government and business, are necessary in order for positive economic growth and prosperity to occur.

Businesses need a well-educated and well-trained workforce, a safe and stable society and a positive economic environment in which to grow and prosper. Government has the primary responsibility of providing the funding and infrastructure necessary to educate and train a workforce; to maintain a safe and stable society, and, to promote a positive economic environment.

Government is not the enemy of prosperity, but low performing government can hinder prosperity. Effective and efficient government promotes prosperity through the provision of a positive economic environment by educating and training a skilled workforce, by providing for public safety; and, by adopting tax policies, strategies, rules and regulations which support the continuation of citizens' prosperity. In order for people to prosper and their quality of life to be improved, government needs businesses to succeed and businesses need efficient government to succeed. It takes effective government and business, working in harmony, to advance the public good and private interests, thereby creating prosperity. A higher quality of life for the people is the result.

Governing Smarter

A new governance performance culture is needed to create the effectiveness and efficiency in government necessary to make the U.S. more competitive, to improve quality of life and to solve 21st century problems. Positive change can come, but it will not be instantaneous. Changing a governance culture is similar to the task of turning a battle ship around in a harbor. It takes time and effort, but it can be done. Specifically, with a new governance approach, government will be able to capture the collective creativity in their workers and citizens necessary to encourage business development; and, create the opportunity for meaningful, permanent, private sector jobs; improve healthcare, reduce crime, improve education, reduce government waste, protect the natural environment, make it easier to do business, reduce domestic violence, make college more affordable and accessible, build new infrastructure, and break the cycle of crime and drugs.

Additionally, with an improved governing culture, government would also be able to create ideas to strengthen families, enhance the potable water supply, support the needs of cities and counties, improve government performance, increase tourism, consolidate government services, and improve cooperation between state and local agencies.

Moreover, with a changed governance culture, government organizations could improve the well-being of children, juvenile justice, create more winners than losers in student testing, reduce incarceration recidivism, become more transparent with the media, develop important achievement goals for government, improve public worker morale, make government more user friendly, and be able to better serve the public's interest above everything else.

Citizens are entitled to government that delivers on its promises; is not wasteful in its spending; has a clear shared vision of what can be accomplished; is value-centered in its decision making, treats people fairly; and, can prove its performance excellence.

Servant Governing provides the energized performance culture necessary to deliver government promises. Servant Governing is the answer to restoring the confidence of the people in government decision making; and, it is the answer to sustained economic improvement. Servant Governing is the answer to meeting the challenges in improving education, job creation, healthcare delivery, children's well-being and improvements to competitiveness and quality of life. Effectiveness and efficiency at all levels of federal, state and local government can be improved through the implementation of the Servant Governing Framework. The people government serves deserve the very best in government effectiveness and efficiency. Servant Governing is the answer the people have been waiting for.

America's future, however, is hanging in the balance if nothing changes. The solutions to our problems can be close at hand. America needs government organizations to be managed in a manner that preserves America's greatness and ensures her competitiveness for today's citizens and for those citizens who will come in the future. After all, is that not the main purpose of one generation, to raise up and prepare the next generation for life and to make things better?

Servant Governing is the governance performance model government leaders and citizens have been looking for because Servant Governing fosters the necessary creativity which is then the source of problem solving ideas for public improvement. Servant Governing also provides the well-spring of management tools needed to identify opportunities and to implement ideas for the improvement of the public good.

Servant Governing is smarter governing. Governing smarter is what the next generation of Americans will be doing, if a correct turn is made now and a new course is set toward real progress. Servant Governing can lead to a smarter, brighter, more secure and sustainable American future for all of her citizens.

"If you do not change direction, you may end up where you were heading."

— LAO TZU

Chapter Two

Servant Governing Defined

- **To Serve the People**
- **Four Cornerstones**

To Serve the People

Victor Hugo is credited with saying, "There is nothing more powerful than an idea whose time has come." The time for Servant Governing in America has come because Americans are in need of real, meaningful, long-term solutions to the challenges it faces.

Servant Governing can first be defined as an embodiment of the primary tenet of a democratic government: To Serve the People. The framers of the U.S. Constitution believed government should be the servant of the people, not their master. Accordingly, in order to properly govern people, government should be wholly committed to serving the people. Service to the people must then be the ultimate objective of any method of democratic governance. Government leaders should be the servants of the citizens. All public servants who work in government must align this commitment to citizen's service with their work activities.

Servant Governing is also defined as an administrative leadership and management framework applicable to government organizations. Servant Governing is not intended for primary application to the legislative or judicial functions of government. Certainly there are the principles of Servant Governing which would be helpful to anyone in public service. However, the main thrust of Servant Governing's application is aimed at executive led government organizations either at the national, state or local level. Servant Governing is also applicable to education institutions, charitable organizations and business organizations in the private sector.

Lastly, Servant Governing can be defined as a leadership and management framework designed to achieve performance excellence. Servant Governing is premised upon four central cornerstones: People, Principles, Priorities and Performance. Each of the Four Cornerstones of the Servant Governing Framework is equally important in creating a people-focused, high-performance, value-centered, problem-solving government organization.

Every government entity, agency or department has some degree of performance expectations. If such government entities, agencies or departments do not meet at least the minimum levels of achievement which are expected, management changes usually will come. Most everyone in government has seen or has experienced the situation where a new leader is brought in to "clean house" and to get things working again. These radical house cleaning efforts often only produce short-term results before mediocrity sets in again. Why? It is because the fundamental nature of the governing culture of the entity, agency or department has not changed.

Servant Governing, on the other hand, brings positive change to a government culture without undermining service to the people in the process. Servant Governing derives its strength for performance excellence from the inherent desire present in most people to do a job well if given the proper support and opportunity. If people are given the proper support, then creativity then begins to flow within the organization. Creativity is a necessary ingredient for performance excellence.

Four Cornerstones

The Four Cornerstones of the Servant Governing work in unison to support a framework for change within a government organization which is seeking to stimulate creativity and achieving performance excellence. The First Cornerstone of the Servant Governing Framework is People, which is premised upon the most effective leadership philosophy and practice proven to encourage creativity and performance excellence: Servant Leadership. Servant leadership is people-focused.

The Second Cornerstone is Principles, which is centered upon core values. Core values guide decision-making and conduct. Adherence to core values promotes good decision-making and ethical behavior by the organization and its people.

The Third Cornerstone is Priorities. When coupled with servant leadership and core values, the establishment of organization mission and vision priorities becomes clearer. Once organizational mission and vision priorities are created, strategic thinking then follows as creativity within the organization emerges. Performance of actions then begins to occur which is consistent with the vision, mission and values of the organization.

The Fourth Cornerstone is Performance, which is powered by motivated people in the organization who are guided by their vision, mission and values in creating strategic priorities which result in actions which are then measured, compared and analyzed.

The Four Cornerstones of Servant Governing are the foundation to support a framework which will ratchet-up the performance of the government organization. Servant Governing is a holistic approach to governing, one which includes a focus on effective leadership of people, defined principles of value, prioritization of strategies and performance measurement analysis. Thus, Servant Governing can be defined as a 21st Century, people focused, value-centered, priority driven, performance-based, public management framework.

When the Servant Governing Framework is implemented, the result is a government organization which stirs creative imagination, stimulates innovation, develops strategies, enhances effectiveness and efficiency, produces real performance results, accomplishes agency goals and objectives; and, delivers better service to the people. Servant Governing provides the leadership philosophy, principles and practice, coupled with the necessary priorities and performance tools to truly serve the public in an effective way.

> "Servant Leadership has been called the most successful leadership strategy in overcoming lackluster employee performances, poor financial results, and executive self interests."
>
> — ART BARTER

Chapter Three

The People Cornerstone

- **Respect and Trust**
- **Servant Leadership**
- **Practical Pointers**

RESPECT AND TRUST

Modern, 21st century servant leaders know and understand that enthusiasm and creativity in the workforce can make the difference between achieving excellence or attaining just mediocre results. The most effective way to stimulate enthusiasm and creativity in the people who make up the workforce and begin the journey toward performance excellence, is a leadership model which first creates a culture of genuine respect and trust among the employees of the workforce and between the organization and those citizens who are being served. Whether the workforce is unionized or not, respect and trust can be engendered, creativity sustained, and performance excellence achieved within a Servant Governance Framework. Respect and trust are the twin pillars which must exist in order for citizens to fully support the government organizations which serve them. The People Cornerstone is the beginning.

There is a plaque hanging on the wall in the F.B.I. Academy in Quantico, Virginia which states:

> "PEOPLE DON'T CARE WHAT YOU KNOW
> WHAT PEOPLE WANT TO KNOW IS, DO YOU CARE?
> IF PEOPLE BELIEVE YOU CARE,
> THEY WILL FOLLOW YOU ANYWHERE."

Caring is essential to creating respect and trust and stimulating creativity within a Servant Governing culture. But caring for whom? Is that all there is? No. There is much more. However, genuine concern and interest by the leader for those around the leader is fundamental. The culture of caring in Servant Governing is created by the leader. The People Cornerstone of Servant Governing is the leadership philosophy and practice of the organization.

SERVANT LEADERSHIP

As stated earlier, the leader in Servant Governing must be a servant leader. Servant leadership is a term coined by Robert K. Greenleaf. Greenleaf's definition of a servant leader is as follows:

> "The servant-leader is servant first... Becoming a servant-leader begins with the natural feeling that one wants to serve, to serve first. Then conscious choice brings one to aspire to lead. That person is sharply different from one who is leader first... The difference manifests itself in the care taken by the servant first to make sure that other people's highest priority needs are being served. The

best test, and the most difficult to administer, is this: Do those served grow as persons? Do they, while being served, become healthier, wiser, freer, more autonomous, more likely themselves to become servants?" (See Greenleaf, R. (1977) *Servant Leadership*, Paulist Press)

The Robert K. Greenleaf Center for Servant Leadership in Westfield, Indiana, was founded upon Robert Greenleaf's philosophy. The purpose of the center is to educate and train people who desire to learn about servant leadership and the servant leader's ability to create respect and trust which can stimulate creativity and effective performance.

Another servant leadership center is the Servant Leadership Institute which was founded by servant-leader Art Barter and is located in Carlsbad, California. The institute provides servant leadership, materials, instruction and books by many well-known authors who have written about servant leadership, including Ken Blanchard, Larry C. Spears, and Dr. Tony Baron.

A third center is the Spears Center for Servant Leadership which was founded by Larry C. Spears who developed a list of ten characteristics of servant leadership which identify a servant leader. These ten characteristics were abstracted from Greenleaf's original writings by Spears who was the former CEO of the Greenleaf Center. The Ten Characteristics of Servant Leadership are:

1. **Listening** – Traditionally, leaders have been valued for their communication and decision making skills. Servant-leaders must reinforce these important skills by making a deep commitment to listening intently to others. Servant-leaders seek to identify and clarify the will of a group. They seek to listen receptively to what is being said (and not said). Listening also encompasses getting

in touch with one's inner voice, and seeking to understand what one's body, spirit, and mind are communicating.

2. **Empathy** – Servant-leaders strive to understand and empathize with others. People need to be accepted and recognized for their special and unique spirit. One must assume the good intentions of coworkers and not reject them as people, even when forced to reject their behavior or performance.

3. **Healing** – Learning to heal is a powerful force for transformation and integration. One of the great strengths of servant-leadership is the potential for healing one's self and others. In "The Servant as Leader" Greenleaf writes, "There is something subtle communicated to one who is being served and led if, implicit in the compact between the servant-leader and led is the understanding that the search for wholeness is something that they have."

4. **Awareness** – General awareness, and especially self-awareness, strengthens the servant-leader. Making a commitment to foster awareness can be scary – one never knows what one may discover! As Greenleaf observed, "Awareness is not a giver of solace – it's just the opposite. It disturbed. They are not seekers of solace. They have their own inner security."

5. **Persuasion** – Servant-leaders rely on persuasion, rather than positional authority in making decisions. Servant-leaders seek to convince others, rather than coerce compliance. This particular element offers one of the clearest distinctions between the traditional authoritarian model and that of servant- leadership. The servant-leader is effective at building consensus within groups.

6. **Conceptualization** – Servant-leaders seek to nurture their abilities to "dream great dreams." The ability to look at a problem (or an organization) from a conceptualizing perspective means that one must think beyond day-to-day realities. Servant-leaders must seek a delicate balance between conceptualization and day-to-day focus.

7. **Foresight** – Foresight is a characteristic that enables servant-leaders to understand lessons from the past, the realities of the present, and the likely consequence of a decision in the future. It is deeply rooted in the intuitive mind.

8. **Stewardship** – Robert Greenleaf's view of all institutions was one in which CEOs, staff, directors, and trustees all play significance roles in holding their institutions in trust for the great good of society.

9. **Commitment to the Growth of People** – Servant-leaders believe that people have an intrinsic value beyond their tangible contributions as workers. As such, servant-leaders are deeply committed to a personal, professional and spiritual growth of each and every individual within the organization.

10. **Building Community** – Servant leaders are aware that the shift from local communities to large institutions as the primary shaper of human lives has changed our perceptions and has caused a feeling of loss. Servant-leaders seek to identify a means for building community among those who work within a given institution.

(Republished with the permission of The Journal of Virtues and Leadership, Vol. 1, Iss. 1, 2010, 25-30; Regent University)

In addition to possessing the foregoing ten characteristics, a servant leader is also fully dedicated to the success of others in the organization and to the citizens the government organization serves. The servant leader believes that the success and growth of those being served is the primary test of a servant leader's effectiveness. Also, the servant leader does not worry about receiving credit. Rather, the servant leader is determined to give credit to others for accomplishments where such credit is due. The servant leader believes in what President Harry S. Truman said, "It's amazing what you can accomplish if you do not care who gets the credit."

The irony of servant leadership is that the true servant leader does not raise his or her hand and say, "Hey! Look at me. I'm a servant leader." Humility is the single most important personality trait in a servant leader. Author Jim Collins, who wrote the book, *Good to Great*, determined through his interviews of great leaders that they all had the common characteristic of humility. That is what makes servant leadership so powerful. The focus is on the leadership being displayed and not on the leader.

The Servant Leadership philosophy and practices have been proven in the private sector. In fact, servant-led organizations in the private sector are more likely to be successful and to produce high performance results. Mr. Art Barter, who is the chairman of Datron World Communications, Inc. and president and C.E.O. of The Servant Leadership Institute in Carlsbad, California, says, "Servant led organizations make more money from a pre-tax standpoint of almost 10 points over and above the S&P 500. Those numbers are generated through a different way of leadership in an organization." (See www.servantleadershipinstitute.com, Video of Art Barter).

As stated, the Servant Leadership Institute holds conferences, offers books, other materials and conducts training sessions to people who are interested in becoming servant leaders. Former Institute President Dr. Tony Baron wrote the book, *The Art of Servant Leadership*, which chronicles the amazing turnaround of Datron World Communications, Inc. under the servant leadership of Art Barter. As evidence in his belief in servant leadership, Art Barter created the Servant Leadership Institute, as a division of Datron, in an effort to transform other organizations by creating servant leaders.

Contrary to the success of servant-led organizations in the private and public sectors, personality-driven, authoritarian and bureaucratic management systems in the private and public sectors do not produce sustained high performance results. In a crisis, or in battle, authoritarian leaders can produce needed short-term results. However, long-term, sustainable, high performance organizational results, even in the military, require a different approach. It is easy to give orders. It is more difficult to ask people what *they* think. In authoritarian cultures, the people who do most of the actual hands-on work spend too much of their time just trying to survive in the culture, rather than being focused on the organization's main mission.

Employees in such traditional, authoritarian management cultures soon learn that as long as employees keep their heads down; keep their opinions to themselves; do not make waves or, do not "rock the boat", they can survive. If the employee does what he or she is told to do, the employee can exist in an authoritarian organizational culture. The problem with such autocratically run organizations in the public sector is that the citizens and employees are usually not engaged in the decision-making or planning within the organization. There is little room for creative idea input. Moreover, public employees in such authoritarian cultures are encouraged to stay in their "silo" and not communicate with others outside their "silo". Consequently, mission focus becomes less of a priority than the employee's own organizational survival in the agency or department.

On the other hand, in servant-led organizations, employee opinions and ideas are valued and sought after. "Servant Leadership is designed to increase the self- determination, self-confidence and self-sacrifice of everyone. Servant Leaders motivate through modeling and proclaiming the importance of service for the sake of others. Giving power away through Servant Leadership will transform individuals and institutions to become empowered and engage the world around them." Dr. Tony Baron. (See Tony Baron, *The Art of Servant Leadership*, Wheatmark Publishers (2013)

Evidence of the concept of servant leadership has been around a long time and can be found in the Old Testament in 1 Kings 12:7: *"Then they spoke to him, saying, 'If you will be a servant to this people today, and will serve them and grant them their petition, and speak good words to them, then they will be your servants forever.'"* (New American Standard Bible) In the New Testament, Jesus Christ said, *"You know that the rulers of the Gentiles lord it over them, their great men exercise authority over them. It is not this way among you; but whoever wishes to become great among you, shall be your servant."* Matthew 20:25-26. (New American Standard Bible)

Robert Greenleaf said,

"The idea of servant is rooted deep in our Judeo-Christian heritage. The concordance to the Standard Revised Version of the Bible lists over 1300 references to servant (including serve and service). Yet, after all of these millennia, there is ample evidence that ours is a low-caring society when judged by what is reasonable and possible with the resources in hand. There are many notable servants among us, but they sometime seem to be losing ground to the neutral or non-serving people. It is argued that the outlook for our civilizations at this moment is not promising, probably because not enough of us care enough for our fellow humans."

(See Robert K. Greenleaf, *The Servant as Leader*.)

The idea of servant leadership is not limited to the Judeo- Christian heritage. It was also revealed in the writing of *Tao Te Ching* which was written in the sixth century BC by Lao Tzu,

"The reason why rivers and seas receive the homage of a hundred mountain streams is that they keep below them. Thus, they are able to reign over all the mountain streams. As the sage, wishing to be above others, stays below them; wishing to be before them, the sage stays behind them. Thus, though the sage be above others, they do not feel the weight; though the sage be before others, they do not count it as an injury."

In a servant governance culture, the servant leader places the citizens and the leader's fellow workers before themselves. The servant leader is not in the government to be served, but to serve. Together, the leader and others in the government serve the citizen-customer. As stated before, in servant governance cultures, giving credit is paramount, not taking credit.

The servant leader considers himself or herself "first among equals" *(Primus Inter Pares)*. The servant leader is "unassuming". The servant leader uses power "honestly". The servant leader "listens". The servant leader "stretches" the people around him. Lastly, a servant leader "adapts" to fit the situation. The result is that the servant leader "enhances the problem-solving skills and abilities of the people in the organization". (See *Servant Leadership: Accepting and Maintaining the Call of Service,* Appendix D hereto.)

If fifty "boots on the ground" are needed in the next ten minutes, authoritarian and servant governance cultures can both deliver. But if fifty new ideas are needed on how to improve the organization, only a servant-led organization can truly deliver. However, servant governance cultures can in some ways require more energy and thought to lead because the leader must be considerate, patient and be willing to listen to others and creatively seek ideas as to how matters can be improved. Even though more effort is sometimes required of the servant leader, the improved results in a servant governance culture are significant as compared to traditionally-led government organizations.

Discipline and order within Servant Governing exists and are maintained not through threat or fear, but through clearly understood values and rules of conduct which are based upon mutual respect, trust and individual responsibility. Servant leaders are not weak. They are at the same time courageous and humble, fair and firm, understanding and determined, caring and resolved. There is great strength in Servant Governing.

The most important people within Servant Governing are the ones who are doing most of the front-line work. For example, in a public safety communications center, the most important persons under Servant Governing would be the persons who answer the 911 call and dispatch the first responder. Supervisors in the communications center are also very important. The value of the supervisors lies in what they know and the experience they have to help serve others. The supervisor would be in turn served by others who also supervise in the organization. As in all cases, true respect and trust by the employee for a supervisor must be earned and cannot be simply ordered.

By turning the Servant Governing organizational pyramid literally upside down, the leader in fact, is shown as the servant of all. The leader as a servant empowers the public workforce and unleashes public employee creativity which is necessary for problem solving within the servant governance organization. People working under Servant Governing have higher morale, are more mission focused and are performance driven. Their energy is not wasted on survival concerns. They know the leader and the organization genuinely cares for the employee.

Under Servant Governing, the 21st century, people-focused, principle-centered, priority-driven, performance-based government organization is then poised for high performance results and success. As stated earlier, the People Cornerstone of servant leadership is the beginning of that journey.

Practical Pointers

1. Commence servant leadership training in your organization. Additional information on servant leadership can be found in Appendices C and D. A list of books, resource materials and information on training classes are also available from The Servant Leadership Institute at www.servantleadershipinstitute.com or from the Robert K. Greenleaf Center for Servant Leadership at www.greenleaf.org.
2. Send members of the staff to servant leadership conferences which are held in Carlsbad, California and Westfield, Indiana through the year.
3. Demonstrate a caring attitude in everything that you do.
4. Be quick to give credit where credit is due.
5. Invert your organizational chart pyramid and explain what it means.
6. Meet with all new employees to discuss the four most important things they need to know: (1) Who the citizen-customer is. (2) The importance of core values. (3) What is a servant- led organization, and (4) Why performance excellence is important.
7. Remember the two major principles of servant leadership:
   a. The employees are not there to serve you; you are there to serve them. Together, the citizen-customer is then served by the organization.
   b. The most important people in the servant- led organization are the ones who do the front line work.
8. Explain to management supervisors that true respect and trust by employees cannot be ordered, it must be earned. In a servant-led organization, supervisors are respected for what they know and who they can help.
9. Use the term "we" when speaking of the organization. Avoid the use of "I" except in giving words appreciation or accepting fault.
10. Do not shirk from the need for employee discipline.

11. Do not overreact when honest, "non-intentional" mistakes are made by employees. Use mistakes as teaching moments.
12. Ask people in the organization what they think. Do this in many different ways to receive employee input. Remember, no one is smart enough to make all the right decisions all the time, or as Ken Blanchard says, "No one is as smart as all of us."
13. Eliminate special parking places for administrators. Give them to employees in recognition of contributions.
14. Get your own coffee. Offer to get coffee for others.
15. Listen to others intently without distractions such as answering cell phones, texting or looking at paperwork on your desk.
16. When possible, sit at a table with those in the organization to discuss matters, not behind a desk.
17. Frequently send handwritten notes to employees in the organization to offer your support, condolences, prayers and congratulations as the situations require.
18. If wages need to be cut, cut your own wages twice as much.
19. If automobiles are furnished as a part of certain positions, do not drive the best one yourself.
20. Make sure others are served first in a serving line before you step in a line, unless you are invited to step forward.
21. Come early and stay late.
22. Speak to everyone in the hallway you meet.
23. Stop and speak to any employee who you run into anywhere outside the premises.
24. Keep people informed as to what is going on in the organization.
25. Keep your promises.
26. Never speak harshly.
27. Laugh often.
28. Never use grievous words or curse words.
29. Never sit when others stand.

30. Ask employees about their family. Follow up on your conversations as required.
31. Dress appropriately. A servant leader is always neat, well groomed and professional in appearance.
32. Do not try to be a "buddy" to any particular employee. A servant leader's responsibility is to serve others. You cannot serve everyone if you are too close to some.
33. At the end of any encounter with an employee, end with this question: "What can I do to help you?", "Do you have everything that you need to do your job?"
34. Recognize acts of servant leadership in others and show your appreciation.
35. Explain important decisions to all employees.
36. Create a recognition system for exemplary work by people in the organization. An informal setting in your office with a couple of supervisors and the employee works just as well as a large ceremony.
37. Remember your role as a servant leader is to help the organization achieve its mission and vision through the growth of others; it is not to receive acclaim for yourself. There is an old adage to remember, "When the tide comes in, all boats will rise, including your own."
38. Encourage community involvement by the organization and its people. Be involved in serving the community yourself.
39. Recognize acts of servant leadership by others within the organization.
40. Don't make servant leadership a mystery.

> *"Be the change that you wish to see in the world."*
>
> — MAHATMA GANDHI

Chapter Four

The Principles Cornerstone

- **Shared Beliefs**
- **Core Values and Ethics**
- **Core Values in a Crisis**
- **Suggested Values**
- **Practical Pointers**

Shared Beliefs

Servant Governing incorporates People as its first cornerstone element in the form of Servant Leadership. Servant Leadership is tremendously impactful and absolutely necessary to transform an organization. Servant Governing not only embodies service to the people through servant leadership, Servant Governing is also based upon shared beliefs. These shared beliefs include an agreed upon set of core values which have been adopted by the organization and which must be adhered to by all persons within the organization. The Principles Cornerstone is core values.

Organizations are never value neutral. When people of value work together, organizational synergism can be a positive result and value-based decisions can be made. However, extreme external pressures on an organization and on individuals can cause previously value-positive people within an organization to resort to value-negative organizational decision making. An example of wide-range value-negative decision making is the Enron scandal of 2001. (See www.whatreallyhappened.com). The only way to ensure consistent, value-positive decision-making on a long-term basis is for the organization itself to adopt agreed upon core values for the organization. It is not enough to assume that because an organization has hired value-centered people, those value-positive decisions will always be made. The organization itself needs to be value-centered.

Adherence to an organization's established core values undergirds employee conduct and ensures consistency of all organizational actions and activities. The core values which need to be agreed upon and adopted by an organization within Servant Governing should be those core values which define people as Americans, as members of the state and local community, as people of character and as members of the organization. Core values are those values which people will not compromise in carrying out their individual employment and citizen responsibilities. Core values define an organization as well.

Core values are those values where intent is essential to their violation. For example, no one can be mistakenly dishonest. If you know what the truth is and you fail to tell the truth, that failure to tell the truth can never be considered as an honest mistake.

Many leading for-profit and not-for-profit organizations are already committed to a set of core values which define their organizations. For example, the Boeing Company believes its core values not only define "... who we are, but also serve as guideposts to help us become the company we would like to be. And, we aspire to live these values every day." (See www.boeing.com). Each branch of the United States military has articulated core values which service men and women live by. (See e.g. www.army.mil/values). Additionally, many government organizations have already established core values to represent the manner in which they conduct business such as the North Carolina Department of Transportation whose core values are: "Safety, customer service, integrity, diversity and quality." (See www.ncdot.gov).

CORE VALUES AND ETHICS

The concepts of core values and ethics are intertwined. Ethics generally refers to behavior. There are many ethics rules governing the conduct of lawyers, doctors, engineers and public officials. Rules prohibiting certain behavior are clearly understood. For example, it would be unethical for a lawyer to discuss his client's confidential business with a third party without the client's approval. A public official generally may not hire his or her own family members to work for the public agency which the official oversees. These are clear ethical standards which prohibit certain conduct.

Core values, on the other hand, are principles of fundamental beliefs which guide and support rules for ethical behavior. Moreover, core values also guide decision-making and conduct where specific ethics rules are not proscribed. For example, it may not be unethical to be lazy or late to a meeting, but such conduct contravenes the values of diligence and punctuality. Core values provide the necessary guidance for all conduct within an organization, especially conduct toward others and the conduct of the organization itself towards others outside the organization.

Core Values in a Crisis

Core values also serve another purpose. Core values help to maintain organizational stability in times of crisis. It is much easier to manage and lead when times are good and everything is going well. It is a much different story when personal or organizational crises arise. When major core value violations and betrayal occur within an organization, it can shake the group to its foundation. Members of the government organization can literally come to a halt in their performance of their duties when a serious core value crisis happens in the organization.

Core value violations will occur in every organization sooner or later. There has only been one perfect person to walk the face of the earth. It is only a matter of time when someone in a government organization will violate the organization's core values. The question is when serious core value violations occur: How does the organization respond?

One thing is certain, if the government organization does not respond when a major core value violation occurs, then the organization risks losing its value-centeredness. Thereafter, decision making within the organization will be at risk for being suspect. Depending on the degree of adversity which arises as a result of major core value violations, it is possible for even a governmental organization to collapse under the weight of disappointment which results from high-ranking misconduct.

However, organizations which are value-centered and have strongly ingrained core values are able to withstand setbacks, including major levels of misconduct by a few. When setbacks occur, it is the core values of the organization which become the focal point; and decisions can then be made to rectify the misconduct which has occurred. The organization and the people in the organization derive strength from their shared belief in their core values. It is the belief in core values which empowers the organization and its people to overcome the organizational assault which arises from major misconduct, betrayal or other catastrophic core value violations.

When times are tough, core values will lead the way out. This is why core values are critical to citizens and to every person within the government organization. The core values which define the organization also empower the organization to make good decisions during a crisis. Core values provide the necessary compass to determine a new direction to overcome the consequences of setback. Core values are not just "feel good" notions which are imagined in ideal circumstances. Rather, core values sustain an organization when hope fades and disintegration appears imminent. Ultimately, it is the core values which will empower the servant leader to energize the people in the organization to not succumb to failure and to chart a new course.

SUGGESTED VALUES

The following are suggested core values which may be considered as examples of values which reflect the ideals inherent in a Servant Governing culture:

Honesty	Professionalism	Fairness
Stewardship	Innovation	Service
Responsiveness	Achievement	Courage
Collaboration	Preparedness	Transparency
Perseverance	Humility	

The suggested examples of Servant Governing core values can be defined as follows:

Honesty
> The qualities of moral excellence, which include truthfulness, fairness in dealing and the absence of fraud and deceit in public service.

Stewardship
> Careful management, protection and trustworthy use of public resources, including people, revenue, infrastructure, investments and the environment.

Achievement
> Accomplishment of public purpose through industrious effort, measurement, analysis and comparison.

Preparedness
> Protecting the public's interest and safety by being ready for anticipated or unexpected events or occurrences, including natural disasters or terrorism; and, by being ready for action through information, planning and practice.

Courage
> Maintaining the quality of mind and mental strength to confront uncertainty and difficulty.

Perseverance
> Continuing a steady effort toward achievement with concern, honesty, patience and endurance despite barriers, difficulties and seeming failures.

Professionalism
> Using the highest degree of skill, training, competence, methods, character and standards in conducting the public's business.

Innovation
> Being creative in the introduction of new ideas, plans and public policy to further the public good.

Service
: Execution of the duties as a servant of the public in a manner beyond what is expected in furtherance of a public purpose.

Transparency
: Conducting public affairs in a candid, open and easily understood manner.

Fairness
: Governing which is free of favoritism or bias; and, being just and equitable, and consistent with rules, logic and ethics.

Responsiveness
: Being willing and ready to answer requests in a timely way and quickly react to conditions, suggestions, appeals and efforts of citizens, the media and other governmental entities.

Collaboration
: Actively working together with others to further the public's interest irrespective of political party, or opposing view, or turf infringement.

Humility
: Giving credit to others for mutual accomplishments and treating others with respect regardless of position.

In summary, defining the core values of the organization is an important step an organization must take in order for it to consistently make good decisions which are essential to creating a culture of performance excellence. The Principles Cornerstone of Core Values and the Servant Leadership Cornerstone provide the first two of the four anchor points for constructing a Servant Governing Framework.

Practical Pointers

1. Adopt a set of core values after receiving full input from all levels of the organization.
2. Prominently display the adopted core values throughout the organization.
3. Ask for volunteers in the organization to write an article about a particular core value; or prepare a video of what the specific core value means to them. Publish the article or show the video at least monthly to all employees about the core value.
4. Refer to your core values in any discipline reports when specific core values have been infringed.
5. Do not make exceptions when it comes to core value violations. Be consistent.
6. Be reasonable in assessing core value infringements.
7. Punctuality is a value. Being five minutes late for a meeting is not a crime. It needs an apology, but it is not the end of the world.
8. Find books on core values and place them in a resource library with servant leadership and other Servant Governing materials. Encourage reading.
9. When it comes to terminating employees for serious core value violations, follow institutional precedents. No one should be terminated for making an unintentional mistake.
10. All decision-making in the organization needs to be consistent with the organization's core values.
11. Review the organization's core values each year and have open discussions concerning them.
12. Remember, the core values you select are representative values. They are not an all inclusive list of important core values.
13. Establish a code of ethics for the organization.

Ethics pertain to behavior. Core values pertain to beliefs. Remember, ethical behavior is based on core values.
14. Speak the truth always.
15. There cannot be two sets of core values; one for the administration and one for the employees. Core values apply to everyone all the time.
16. When core value violations occur within a government organization, immediately notify the media. Transparency with the public and with the media further engenders the respect and trust necessary for effective governance. The people being served by government have a right to know what is going on. This fundamental right of the people is safeguarded by the media. Only issues involving security should be withheld, but only for a reasonable time.

> "You have to decide what your highest priorities are and have the courage – pleasantly, smilingly, nonapologetically – to say 'no' to other things. And the way to do that is by having a bigger 'yes' burning inside."
>
> — DR. STEPHEN R. COVEY

Chapter Five

The Priorities Cornerstone

- **WIGS**
- **Mission and Vision**
- **Priority Goals (WIGS)**
- **Strategy Opportunities**
- **Strategic Planning**
- **Practical Pointers**

Following the implementation of the People and Principles Cornerstones, the Priorities Cornerstone of the Servant Governing Framework is the next step in envisioning the future and developing strategies to achieve that future. The Priorities Cornerstone reflects the innovation of the organization and its commitment to achieving performance excellence. The establishment of the organization's priorities and the strategies to achieve those priorities are given serious attention within a servant governance culture.

WIGS

The late Dr. Stephen R. Covey advised his followers to do a few things to achieve excellence, rather than doing many things and being satisfied with mediocrity. Dr. Covey recommended focusing on a few "widely important goals" (WIGS) and setting aside items which can be described as being "merely important".
(See http://www.franklincovey.com/tc/solutions/business-execution-solutions/the-4-disciplines-of-execution-manager-certification/objectives).

Dr. Covey's original instruction on WIGS is central to Servant Governing's Cornerstone of Priorities. The question which needs to be asked is this: What are the broad goals of the organization which must be accomplished or maintained even if nothing else is achieved? When the needs of the citizens are distilled into a few guiding statements of long-term public goals, those statements of goals will serve as a guide for specific shorter-term strategy development as the organization works to achieve those broader goals.

MISSION AND VISION

However, prior to establishing an organization's broad goals, the organization's mission and vision need to be created with careful consideration. Servant Governing not only embodies service to the people through servant leadership and adherence to defining core values, Servant Governing is also based upon an understood purpose of the organization which is articulated through a clear statement of the organization's mission.

All organizations of people need an understood mission focus in order to be effective. Government agency and department organizations are no exception. The people who work in an organization, work better, smarter and more creatively when the organization's purpose is clear and the worker believes his or her effort each day is actually furthering the mission of the organization.

In addition to having an agreed upon and understood mission, high performance organizations should articulate a shared vision of what the organization could be in the future. The vision and mission of the organization provide the necessary "North Star" which then permits alignment of an organization's goals, actions, activities, plans and operations with the mission and vision. The statement of mission and vision of the organization should clearly answer two questions:

(1) What is the main purpose of the organization; and
(2) With hard work and focus, what could the organization be in the future?

Set forth below are the examples of vision and mission statements of a government organization, which would be the first step in establishing the necessary priorities focus within the Servant Governing Framework:

Vision Statement

A state (county or city) achieves a most desirable level of public safety and quality of life for all its citizens because it has:
- servant governance and premier agency performance
- a highly trained public and private sector workforce
- equal and fair opportunity and justice
- world-class K-12 education
- most envied child well-being
- a reputation for business success

- unmatched economic opportunity and prosperity
- innovative ideas and policies
- unparalleled recreational value to residents and visitors and
- a sustainable natural environment

Mission Statement

We, as public servants of the people, will:
- serve with honor
- utilize value-centered, high performance leadership and management practices
- provide excellent service to our citizens, businesses, families, and visitors
- be transparent and responsive to everyone, including the media and other government entities
- be effective, safe and efficient stewards of all resources, and the environment
- in accordance with our constitution and law

Priority Goals (WIGS)

In addition to the adoption of clear statements of mission and vision, the Priority Cornerstone of the Servant Governance Framework also includes the need to establish the most important priority goal accomplishments or improvements which need to be made if a government entity is to become world-class. In order to make a better future for citizens achievable and sustainable, the Priorities Cornerstone of the Servant Governing Framework is designed to provide the necessary focus for implementing strategies, actions and initiatives.

In most cases, priority goals for a state or locality fall into five major categories. Typically, all government entities need to address one or more of these priority goals which are set forth in the five important categories below. The following are suggested examples of what Dr. Covey refers to as WIGS or priority goals which would be used to prioritize actions, strategies and initiatives in a government organization:

1. Governing
   Government's most solemn obligation to the people is public safety, which includes reducing crime, especially crimes against seniors, women and children; and includes maintaining a high degree of homeland security and emergency management preparedness. The people are entitled to servant governance and high government performance results.

2. Quality of Life
   The people are entitled to a quality of life which includes safe schools and neighborhoods, access to excellent healthcare, expanded economic opportunity, affordable, well-planned housing, a family friendly environment, good roads, modern transportation, abundant recreational opportunities and active, peaceful retirement opportunities.

3. Education
   The people are entitled to the opportunity to attend excellent and safe schools; to be ready for college or career; to be able to access and to afford higher education or to receive advanced workforce training and technical knowledge. Teachers need to be compensated fairly. Schools must have appropriate funding. Comprehensive testing of student and school performance must be reasonable, fair and not overshadow learning.

4. Employment

    The people are entitled to have meaningful job opportunity creation in order to support themselves and their families in manufacturing, medical services, education, technology, agriculture, construction, aerospace, government, retail and service industries. Businesses are entitled to have a positive economic and governmental environment in which to successfully compete and profitably grow in a global market; and be able to create good paying jobs for well-trained, highly motivated and satisfied workers.

5. Plan for Growth

    The people are entitled to a growth strategy which protects the natural environment, including oceans, lakes, rivers, springs and canals; which enhances potable water supply, expands recreation and tourism; ensures hospital and medical service; develops new transportation systems, roads and parks; and which reduces electricity consumption and increases renewable energy, encourages quality residential/commercial development; and, which creates a more sustainable future for the people.

STRATEGY OPPORTUNITIES

Within each of the five suggested examples of broad goals within the Priorities Cornerstone are many specific examples of issues which could serve as opportunities for improvement in government performance. Examples of specific opportunities for improvement which could be further prioritized and made a part of a strategic plan could be called "Smart Strategies."

Smart Strategies have five aspects:

1. Specific
2. Measurable
3. Attainable
4. Responsible
5. Time specific

Suggested Smart Strategies include:

1. Governing
   Smart Safe Communities and Schools ... Smart Public Safety Agency Support ... Smart Counter Terrorism ...Smart Drug policy ... Smart Violent crime Reduction Plan ... Smart Citizen Sourcing ... Smart State and Local Collaboration ... Smart Regulation and Permitting ... Smart Prison Reentry Reform ... Smart Budget Planning ... Smart Agency Services Consolidation ... Smart State-Local Government Cooperation .... Smart Sales Tax Fairness ... Smart Vehicle Purchase and Maintenance ... Smart Retirement System Fairness ... Smart Government Process Improvement Methods ... Smart Juvenile Justice Reform ... Smart Cargo Theft Prevention ... Smart Water, Waste and Energy Policy ... Smart Regulation Review.

2. Quality of Life
   Smart Active Lifestyle ... Smart Sustainable Communities ... Smart Child Well-Being ... Smart Government and Faith Community Collaboration ... Smart Healthcare Access ... Smart Urban Development and Redevelopment ... Smart Home Foreclosure Reform ... Smart Alternative Fuel Use ... Smart Senior Enrichment ... Smart Homeless Reduction ... Smart

Family and Youth Programs ... Smart Farm Protection ... Smart Volunteerism ... Smart Obesity Prevention...Smart Domestic Violence Reduction.

3. Education
Smart Early learning and Pre-K... Smart Safe Schools, Common Core Standards and Race To The Top ... Smart Testing Reform ... Smart College and University System ... Smart Career Development ... Smart K-20 Curriculum ... Smart Work Force Training Collaboration ... Smart Professional Development ... Smart College Affordability ... Smart Graduate Retention ... Smart Life-Long Learning.

4. Employment
Smart Diversification of Business...Smart Hi Tech Innovation Incubation ... Smart and Skilled Work Force ... Smart International Connections ... Smart Development of Existing Manufacturing "Nodes"... Smart Productivity Improvement ... Smart Job Creation and Nurturing ... Smart Public Sector and Private Sector Workforce Appreciation and Recognition ... Smart Workforce Development and Training.

5. Plan for Growth
Smart Business Prosperity Policies ... Smart Economic Incentives ... Smart Tourist Initiative ... Smart Recreation, Bike Paths and State Park Expansion ... Smart New Statewide Celebrations ... Smart Rail Transportation ... Smart Road Planning and Construction ... Smart Permitting for Business Expansion and Housing Development ... Smart Environment Sustainment ... Smart Land Use Planning.

Strategic Planning

Under the Priorities Cornerstone of the Servant Governing Framework, identifying strategies to accomplish broad goals requires a planning process that needs to be well-developed and meaningful. Strategic plans of the past are outmoded today. Traditional, long-term strategic planning typically had a planning horizon of five years or more. Long-term planning horizons were based upon a post-World War II mindset in which past events were good predictors of what the future may hold. This idea of the past predicting the future was grafted into the business world and strategic planning became business "buzz" words. Often, however, strategic plans became nothing more than books which gathered dust on the shelf and were of little value.

Today, the world is much different. The internet is a great resource tool and it has made good data easy to obtain. Communication is instantaneous. In many respects, the world has become so fast-paced that a good idea today may be obsolete tomorrow. Almost overnight, someone can put a good idea into action and literally launch a new business – and be very successful at it. In view of the change in today's world, some argue that long-term strategic planning is useless because the future is so uncertain. As a result, many organizations have given up trying to predict the future through a long-term strategic plan. (See *The Strategic Plan is Dead* by Dana O'Donovan and Noah Fowler, Jan. 29, 2013. Stanford Social Innovation Review, Vol. 11, No. 2.)

However, while it may be true that the static, traditional, long-term strategic plan is outmoded, there is a critical need for vibrant, shorter term, focused, data-driven strategic thinking, especially in government. Roads must still be built, schools must be planned, and the environment must be protected. The importance of essential government functions and the delivery of government services in a changing world require a road map for action. That road map or strategic plan can be an effective tool for leading and managing in a changing world under challenging conditions.

The threat of terrorism has changed the way the military develops strategies in order to meet new threat conditions. Likewise, non-military organizations need to maintain their agility as well. Maintaining agility is paramount, but not at the expense of critical strategy planning. Supreme Allied Commander and President of the United States Dwight D. Eisenhower once said, "Plans are useless, but planning is everything."

Without planning, an organization may spend its time and use its peoples' energy just trying to cope with day-to-day problems. That kind of organization becomes reactive instead of strategic. Over time, a reactive organizational culture based on crisis management, will eventually lead to perpetual mediocre performance, or worse.

Therefore, strategic thinking and planning are a critical element of the Priorities Cornerstone of the Servant Governing Framework. Strategic thinking which arises in a servant-led organization, coupled with powerful commitment to mission and vision, will generate positive organizational action. Strategic planning causes the organization to look into the future to determine how its vision and mission are to be achieved consistent with its values. The vision and mission of an organization cannot be achieved without strategic planning and action. Accountability for action is what drives progress. The need to make progress stimulates the creativity needed for ideas for strategy development.

Once an organization adopts a set of broad priority goals, specific measurable objectives and action steps can be designed to implement those goals. Achievable strategies can be created, assigned, measured and reviewed. Achievements of strategies should be communicated and celebrated. The new levels of performance achievements can become "benchmarks" for future performance measurement and accountability.

Government organizations which face long-term and chronic societal problems must remain steadfast and patient in developing strategic plans. Therefore, a reasonable balance of longer-term goals and shorter-term goals should be included in a government organization's strategic plan. Longer-term goal planning is necessary and acceptable as long as there are shorter-term steps being made and accomplished toward the ultimate goal. In high performance organizations, long-range forecasting is typically translated into shorter-term operating plans.

The Priorities Cornerstone of the Servant Governing Framework creates the strategies for action by the organization. Armed with specific strategies, the people within the servant-led, value-centered organization are ready to demonstrate performance.

Practical Pointers

1. If the organization has not articulated its mission and vision, begin the process with sessions with employees to create a written statement of purpose of the organization and its possible future.
2. Ask employees to write down how they can further the purpose in the employee's daily work.
3. Next, begin to fashion a clear statement of mission which should include the purpose and major aspects of work which further the purpose.
4. After the mission is established, conduct "visionary" sessions with employees to determine what the organization could be in the future with hard work and good fortune.
5. Finalize a vision for the organization which describes the organization's future highest potential.
6. Develop a process for establishing a strategic plan for the organization.
7. Involve as much of the organization as possible in the strategic planning process.
8. Start the strategic planning process with a group discussion of the organization's Strengths, Weaknesses, Opportunities and Threats. This is called a SWOT analysis.
9. Senior management should outline the organization's most important guiding strategies or Widely Important Goals (WIGS).
10. WIGS guide the development of specific strategies for organizational improvement which all strategic planning must address.
11. Every strategy should have at least two objectives which are specific and designed to accomplish the strategy.
12. Each adopted strategy should have at least two action steps which are specific courses of action which are to be taken to further the strategy.
13. Every action step must be measurable.

14. Every action step must have in writing the person who is to be responsible and the date the action step is to be accomplished.
15. Planning horizons can vary, but the most progress will be made with shorter horizons. A one-year plan is a good plan.
16. A strategic plan is a flexible document and can be amended and revised.
17. A strategic plan should be aligned with the organizations vision, mission, values and organizational goals.
18. A strategic plan should be reviewed at least quarterly by the CEO in a meeting devoted to the strategic plan review.
19. Every division of the organization should have strategic planning objectives it is trying to accomplish.
20. A strategic planning session should be held to finalize the strategic planning objectives and action steps.
21. At the end of each year, a formal strategic plan review of every action step should be undertaken. Any action step which has not been completed should be either rolled-over to the following year, or abandoned by the senior leadership based on justifiable reasons.
22. People in the organization should be encouraged to stretch the organization and themselves.
23. People should not be punished for stretching to reach a goal, if they did not make the goal. Always be reasonable. A strategic plan is not a trap for the unwary.
24. Share the strategic plan in as much detail as possible with the public and with the media.
25. Recognize strategic plan accomplishments often.
26. Prioritization of strategic planning goals should be based upon citizen customer input and need, including input from volunteers.

"To improve is to change; to be perfect is to change often."

— WINSTON CHURCHILL

Chapter Six

The Performance Cornerstone

- ❋ CRITERIA
- ❋ ORGANIZATIONAL TRANSFORMATION
- ❋ PRACTICAL POINTERS

CRITERIA

The last Cornerstone of the Servant Governing Framework is Performance. Servant Governing envisions a management framework which, when implemented, would capture the creativity and collective energy of employees and direct their creativity and energy toward performance excellence. The Performance Cornerstone elements within the Servant Governing Framework are based upon the Florida Sterling Council's Criteria for Performance Excellence. The 2013 Sterling Criteria are included in Appendix A and serve as a guide to achieving performance excellence. Many states, including Florida, have adopted the Malcolm Baldridge National Quality Award Criteria. Florida is a leading example of the use of the performance management criteria in government and in business in order to achieve performance excellence.

The Performance Cornerstone is where the "rubber meets the road." In the last analysis, positive government organizational results should always be a goal to be achieved. Important measurements of organizational results should be adopted and maintained. It is the proof of organizational performance. Analysis of results should also include a comparison of the organization's results with other similar government entities. In every instance, comparable peer organization data can be ascertained for comparison purposes. Final numbers are not the end all of assessment of human endeavor. Courage, compassion, persistence and humility cannot be measured in numbers. However, almost everything else government does for the people it serves, can be measured.

ORGANIZATIONAL TRANSFORMATION

There is an adage to remember: "If it's important, measure it. If you measure it, compare it. If you compare it, develop a strategy to make it better." In order to obtain the desired results in government organizational activity, deployment of the Servant Governing Performance Cornerstone elements must occur. The Performance Cornerstone elements include Citizen-Customer Service, Employee Empowerment, Operational Improvement, Key Measurements and Results Scoreboards:

Citizen-Customer Service

Customer Service is generally referred to as activities designed to enhance the level of customer satisfaction. Typically, customer service refers to a service or the provision of a product before, during and after purchase.

A relatively new concept in government is that citizens are customers, too. In business, customers who do not receive expected customer service have the option of getting their money back, or taking their business to another store. Citizens should be viewed as "customers" of government because citizens pay taxes in one manner or another to the government which serves them. In effect, citizens buy government services with their tax dollars. Therefore, citizens are entitled to be treated as " customers" of the government service.

The difference between customers of a business and citizen-customers of government is that in business, customers can get a return of their money when a product fails or where service is inadequate. Citizen-customers of government cannot get their money back. In addition, business customers can take their business somewhere else, while citizen-customers do not have that luxury. Accordingly, citizen-customers deserve the highest degree of customer satisfaction because their choices are limited.

Within Servant Governing, Citizen-Customer Service can always be improved and should be monitored continually. Citizen-Customer feedback is imperative to effective Servant Governing. This allows the organization to focus its attention in the key areas, measured by the right key performance indicators. Examples of Citizen-Customer Service feedback or "listening posts" are included in Appendix B.

Employee Empowerment

Generally, "Employee Empowerment" is a term that is used to express the different ways line level employees of an organization can make decisions without consulting their bosses or managers. Within Servant Governing, employee empowerment is necessary in order to generate creativity which is then the fuel for attaining performance excellence. Employee empowerment not only gives power to individuals, it makes for more satisfied employees. Employees become more vested in the organization. Greater feelings of self-worth by employees is a result of employee empowerment.

Employee Empowerment is a strategy and a philosophy that enables employees to do their work and to take responsibility for their own results. Ultimately, Employee Empowerment results in better Citizen-Customer Service at every level of the organization. Employee Empowerment also involves team building, delegation of authority and responsibility. Within Servant Governing, Employee Empowerment cures many organizational ills and leads to a great potential for performance excellence if done in the right manner. Various examples of ways to empower employees are described in Appendix B.

Operational Improvement

An important part of the Performance Cornerstone is the concept of Operational Improvement which is comprised of formal and informal steps to improve operational processes within the government organization. A "process" is the way in which things are done. Every function within a government organization usually has a process attached to it. The simple mailing of a letter has a process which has been developed over time. Within Servant Governing, there is a constant focus on improving operational processes in the organization.

The Operational Improvement focus is designed to introduce process changes that will improve the quality of the government service rendered. Employees within the organization, which has implemented Servant Governing, are empowered to make process changes which contribute to improvement and performance excellence. Examples of Operational Improvement methods are described in Appendix B.

Key Measurements

Another important part of the Performance Cornerstone is the Key Measurements which must be made within the organization to determine whether progress is being made toward targeted goals. Key Measurements are quantifiable measurements; agreed to within the organization to measure performance. Within Servant Governing, Key Measurements reflect the government organization's progress toward performance excellence. Examples of Key Measurements are set forth in Appendix B.

Results Scoreboards

Lastly, and an equally important element of the Performance Cornerstone is the focus on results. The Results Scoreboards is a term which reflects the reporting of performance measures as compared to targeted measurements. Results Scoreboards can be depicted in many ways throughout the organization and should be placed in prominent places for all employees to see. A common denominator of all presentation methods is that it helps employees and managers to focus attention on strategy implementation and measurement of progress toward stated goals. For example, trends of past performance can be measured and compared to current performance and desired targeted performance levels. Comparison with best peer organizations can also be made and analyzed in graph form.

As previously stated, specific examples of the actual implementation of the five elements of the Performance Cornerstone, including Results Scoreboards, can be found in Appendix B. The criteria upon which each element of the Performance Cornerstone is based is fully set forth in Appendix A. Taken together, the Four Cornerstones of the Servant Governing Framework comprise the foundation and structure for the construction of a high-performance government organization. The Performance Cornerstone contains the elements of quantifiable proof which can be relied upon to determine whether the desired performance progress is being made.

Practical Pointers

1. Establish meaningful performance measures for every department and division within the organization. Ask the employees which measures are important to them and which measures will help them in their work.
2. Update performance measures daily or weekly as required.
3. Establish at least ten key performance indicators for the entire organization. Update the key performance indicators at least monthly with senior management.
4. Track key performance indicators over a number of years to determine trends. Establish best peer benchmarks for key performance indicators and compare the benchmarks to organizational trends.
5. Develop scoreboards for displaying appropriate performance measurements and key performance indicators; throughout the respective departments of the organization.
6. Establish a method to visually assess whether key performance indicators are trending in an acceptable manner. For example, the use of a traffic light with red, yellow and green lights on the scoreboard gives a quick reference as to whether the trend is acceptable and is on track to meet expected targets.
7. Develop a STAT process pertaining to every important measurement within the organization. At least quarterly, senior management should meet with each department for a STAT review. The STAT review process should not be an adversary process. The CEO and senior management in attendance should always be encouraging concerning performance. Never manage through fear.
8. Develop quality review teams comprised of line level employees which are established to review operational processes of the organization.

9. Empower employees to make recommended changes in processes. The quality review team should meet regularly and should have a line- level chairperson of the team.
10. Chairpersons of quality review teams should meet with the CEO and senior management at least quarterly to determine the progress of the quality review teams throughout the organization.
11. Train employees in the concepts of various process improvement techniques such as Lean Six Sigma and Rapid Process Improvement.
12. Create an employee incentive rewards program for employee suggestions and ideas for cost reduction.
13. Conduct regular anonymous employee surveys.
14. Conduct citizen customer surveys on organizational performance.
15. If employee surveys show a deficiency, request senior management to develop a corrective plan. Share the information with all employees.
16. Look for the good in everyone. Forgive the mistakes of the past. Do not harbor grudges. Do not punish your enemies and only reward your friends.
17. Great assistance is available through the Florida Sterling Council which can be accessed through the Florida Sterling Council's website: www.floridasterling.com
18. Additional assistance can be acquired through organizations such as Active Strategy, a software and consulting company whose software creates scoreboards (dashboards, scorecards) for use in the organization.
    (See www.activestrategy.com).

"You miss 100 percent of the shots you never take."

— WAYNE GRETZKY

Chapter Seven

The Sailboat Analogy

- **Sailboat Components**
- **Servant Governing Components**

Sailboat Components

Often a simple analogy can be used to explain new concepts. An analogy which compares the interdependence of a sailboat's components with the interdependence of Servant Governing's Cornerstone components is particularly useful.

A sailboat is unique in that it is comprised of a multitude of interdependent components which allow the craft to move through the water toward the predetermined destination. In order to have an effective sailing vessel, all of the components must be working together in harmony. The captain and crew must be well-trained; must know the destination; and must fully understand the functions of the various sailboat components in order to make a safe journey.

Likewise, the Servant Governing Framework has interdependent cornerstone elements. When the cornerstone elements are implemented together and are working in harmony, the Servant Governing

Framework will cause the governmental organization to make its journey toward performance excellence in a measurable way.

The components of a typical sailboat include a keel, which stabilizes the craft no matter how difficult the challenges which are ahead; or, even how dangerous are the challenges presently being encountered. The sailboat's bow always points in the direction in which the sailboat is heading. The bow is designed to achieve the desired performance. The sails power the craft steadily to its destination. The compass and instruments allow for measurement of progress and indicate whether the sailboat is on course for its destination. The helm allows the craft to be steered. The rudder, of course, responds to the helm and causes the sailboat to head in the right direction. Lastly, the hull provides the structure of the sailboat and ties all the components together to enable the craft to accomplish its purpose.

When taken together, the interdependent components of the sailboat work together to enable the vessel to safely make the journey to the desired destination. Lastly, and most importantly, the captain and crew work together to operate the sailboat. Under direction of the captain and crew, the vessel is able to safely make the journey.

Servant Governing Components

The Servant Governing Framework contains interdependent cornerstone elements which directly relate to the functional components of the sailboat, captain and crew in the following ways:

1. People Cornerstone:

The captain and crew represent the servant leader and workforce of the organization which are needed for function, control and performance. The leadership component in a Servant Governing Framework is based upon servant leadership.

2. Principles Cornerstone:

The keel, which stabilizes the sailboat, represents the Servant Governing's core values which are essential in providing stability to decisions. No matter what the challenge the government organization is facing, adherence to its core values will keep the organization and its employees steadily moving in the right direction regardless of the turbulence the organization may encounter.

3. Priorities Cornerstone:

The helm represents the vision, mission, and goals of the organization which must be established in the servant governance culture; and they are required in order to have an understanding of the purpose for which the organization exists and the ultimate achievements the organization should be able to attain on behalf of the people.

The rudder responds to the helm and is symbolic of strategic planning. Without a well-developed, modern strategic plan which is deployed throughout the government organization in an appropriate manner, neither the people in the organization, nor the citizens will know where the organization is heading or how it is going to get there.

The bow represents Citizen-Customer Service which a governmental organization should have as its primary focus if it is to make headway.

4. Performance Cornerstones:

The first sail represents the Employee Empowerment component which is necessary to harness the creativity within the public workforce and which makes the organization more fully energized, thereby creating success.

The second sail of the sailboat represents the harnessed energy of the government's Operational Improvement of organizational procedures which set forth the manner, method, policies and procedures of doing business. Continuous, sustained, operational process improvement is essential to achieving performance excellence under Servant Governing.

The compass relates to Key Measurements and analysis which the organization must have in order to know whether progress is being made toward the stated goals. The measurements are analyzed and compared to assist planning and decision making within the Servant Governing culture.

Lastly, all the components of the sailboat are tied together by the hull. Similarly, all the Cornerstones of the Servant Governing Framework, working together in an organization which is fully committed to Servant Governing, will cause the organization to have positive organizational results. The measure of success is excellent governmental results and service to its citizens. Results Scoreboards are needed to inform all stakeholders of the desired performance level and whether performance targets are being achieved.

The sailboat analogy is designed to depict the Four Cornerstones of the Servant Governing Framework as interdependent components of a public management framework which will increase government organizational performance when implemented together. (See Figures 1 and 2).

SAILBOAT ANALOGY

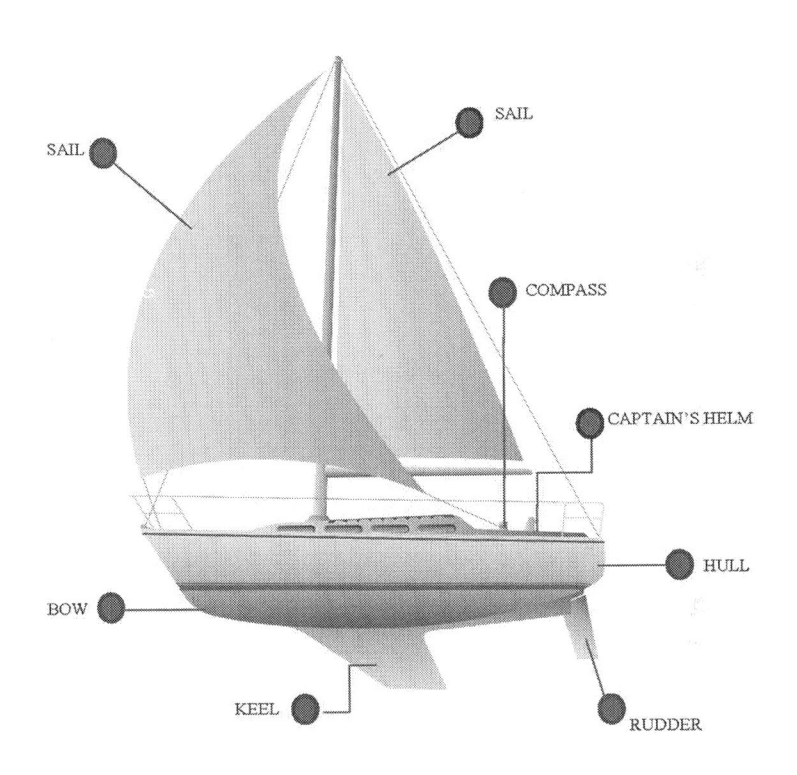

Figure 1

SAILBOAT ANALOGY

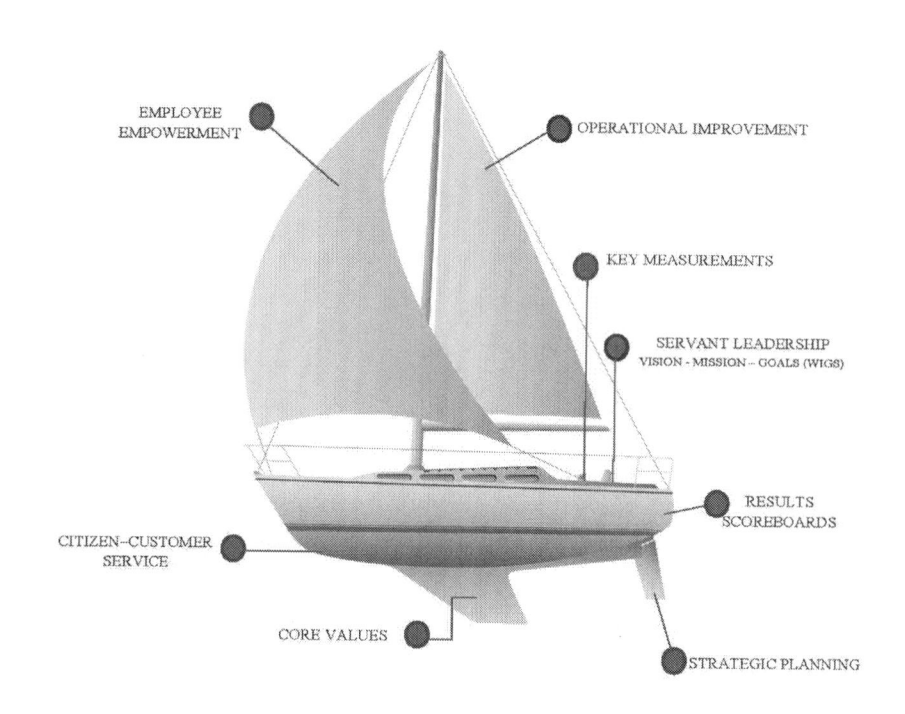

- EMPLOYEE EMPOWERMENT
- OPERATIONAL IMPROVEMENT
- KEY MEASUREMENTS
- SERVANT LEADERSHIP
  VISION – MISSION – GOALS (WIGS)
- RESULTS SCOREBOARDS
- CITIZEN–CUSTOMER SERVICE
- CORE VALUES
- STRATEGIC PLANNING

SERVANT GOVERNING FRAMEWORK

PEOPLE CORNERSTONE: Servant Leadership
PRINCIPLES CORNERSTONE: Core Values
PRIORITIES CORNERSTONE: Vision
Mission
Goals (WIGS)
Strategic Planning
PERFORMANCE CORNERSTONE: Citizen – Customer Service
Employee Empowerment
Operational Process Improvement
Key Measurements
Results Scoreboards

Figure 2

> *"The most serious problem in leadership is not the lack of leaders, but the misuse and abuse of applied power. We have many leaders, but they are the wrong kind."*
>
> — TONY BARON

Chapter Eight

Conclusion

This book began with the question, "What are we trying to accomplish?" A way to achieve excellence in government performance was the answer. The premise throughout this writing has been that Americans deserve better than the mediocre government performance which has thus far been realized in the areas of education, economic opportunity, healthcare, children's well-being and in high-skill job creation. While some advancement has occurred in certain of these areas, challenges remain and improved performance has not been achieved in all of the areas that matter to most citizens.

Servant Governing is an "idea whose time has come." Benjamin Franklin's theory that government should be the servant of the people, not their master, is best embodied in the Servant Governing Framework. Servant Governing is based upon people leadership, adherence to principles, the development of priorities and the measurement of performance. Servant Governing empowers people to do well, to creatively solve problems through new ideas and to seize the opportunities to overcome challenges. The Servant Governing Framework for action will deliver the high performance results sorely needed in America in order to meet the challenges of the future.

The Four Cornerstones of the Servant Governing Framework will capture the creativity and collective energy of government organizations and direct that creativity and energy toward achieving high performance excellence. Adoption of the Servant Governing Framework will transform any government entity into a 21st Century high performance leader in areas that matter most to Americans, including public safety, economic opportunity, quality education, a clean environment and a superior quality of life.

Businesses which have the ability to create meaningful, high paying and permanent employment will be attracted to high performance states and localities as a place in which to locate and expand their operations. The reason? High performing, 21st Century businesses want to do business in an area where government is also guided by high performance, 21st Century creative strategies, leadership and government results. High performance businesses and their leaders and workers know they can prosper in a state which has an effective and efficient government culture which,

(1) operates world-class schools, colleges and universities;
(2) produces career ready students;
(3) provides world-class workforce education and training;
(4) supports the development of first-rate, safe residential communities and schools; and
(5) promotes quality recreational opportunities unmatched anywhere else.

In other words, high performance government results in a high performance economy which, in turn, increases the quality of life and the well-being of the citizens. This triangular, interdependent relationship between quality governance, substantial economic growth and improved well-being of citizens is the formula for achieving a successful future for all citizens.

Performance excellence can only be achieved by a government organization which is willing to implement an integrated approach to organizational performance management. The Servant Governing

Framework is the proven, integrated approach to achieving organizational performance excellence which will improve government effectiveness, accountability and value to citizen-customers.

Many government leaders have been searching for a better government performance and management model with which to solve problems. One example is Maryland Governor Martin O'Malley who has led his state through the Great Recession with outstanding results by utilizing high performance management tools. Governor O'Malley was formerly the Mayor of Baltimore where he instituted a performance measurement called "CittiStat" which received the "Innovations in Government" award from Harvard University's John F. Kennedy School of Government. Later, Governor O'Malley instituted "StateStat" when he became Governor of Maryland. Maryland has achieved significant gains in its economy and education system as a result of Governor O'Malley's performance measurement and management emphasis. In 2009, Governor O'Malley was named Governing Magazine's "Official of the Year".

Another example is in Alabama. The State of Alabama has adopted a statewide strategic planning system using the acronym SMART which stands for Specific results, Measurable goals, Accountable, Responsive and Transparent.

On a local level, in Marion County, Florida, the Marion County Sheriff's Office began its Servant Governing performance excellence journey in 1998 which culminated in the Sheriff's Office receiving the 2008 "Governor's Sterling Award" for performance excellence from the Florida Sterling Council. In 2011, the Marion County Sheriff's Office received the "Sustained Excellence Award" from the Florida Sterling Council for continued performance excellence. The Marion County Sheriff's Office was the first law enforcement agency in Florida to be recognized for achieving performance excellence based upon the Malcolm Baldridge National Quality Criteria and the Florida Sterling Council's Criteria for Performance Excellence.

The question which remains as to whether Servant Governing can be implemented is, "Do the citizens and their leaders have the collective will to change?" The people are only limited by how strongly citizens and their leaders believe change is necessary. The indomitable, positive American spirit is still alive and well within its people. It just needs to be stirred into action and work. President Theodore Roosevelt said, "Far and away the best prize that life offers is the chance to work hard at work worth doing."

Negative thinking appears to be permeating politics in this country. America needs patriotic optimists to counter the pessimism which hinders change for the better in government performance. In a 2012 article, Editorial Page Editor, Brad Rogers, of the Ocala, Florida Star Banner weighed in on the issue of negative thinking in politics.

"One annoying characteristic of 21st Century American political platforms is that they are almost uniformly built on what our wannabe elected representatives are against. They are against taxes, against government, against spending and too often, amazingly, against compromise on any of those things other than things they are against." (Used by permission)

Mr. Rogers then issued a challenge to men and women who seek public office, "Be 'for' something, anything that will make our county better, stronger, more beautiful, more prosperous, more educated, more livable." Mr. Rogers has hit the nail on the head.

Citizens and their leaders throughout this magnificent nation need to collectively capture a spirit of determined and united progress once again. America is capable of being much better than the so-so rankings it has received in important quality of life measurements in comparison to other industrialized nations. After all, this is America, the leader of the free world.

Creative ideas are needed to overcome those negative rankings which have resulted primarily from mediocre performance in government.

Citizens and their leaders need to envision an attainable and brighter future for all Americans and do something about it through the implementation of the Servant Governing Framework. With God's help it can and must be done.

EPILOGUE

Compromise: Issue or Value

I asked some of my family members to review a draft manuscript of *Servant Governing*. There was one comment which I received which I decided to explore in this epilogue. A question was raised whether Servant Governing can be effective and still produce results in a time when political intolerance and extreme divergence of political opinion seem to be growing. How can there be effective governance in society where compromise has become a "dirty word"?

There are certainly some who believe "to compromise, is to fail". As a result, some people believe gridlock has overtaken our national political discourse. Even some others maintain that the increasing polarization of political discussion has been unnecessarily increased on both sides of issues by pundits on talk radio and cable television. Notwithstanding all the negativity and sharp partisan divide which often exists regarding public policy issues, I strongly contend Servant Governing is effective and has proven itself in ameliorating public policy differences.

I have observed over the years that intractability on public policy issues occurs, and political tension between people continues, not just because of unreasonableness. More often, gridlock occurs as a result of people's misunderstanding of the difference between value compromise and issue compromise. Specifically, a distinction needs to be drawn between compromising one's own core values and compromising on issues. The latter is an integral, necessary, reasonable and natural part of consensus building.

A person should not be expected to compromise their core values. Core values should be respected by others, except when such values are based upon negative or destructive beliefs such as hatred, envy, inequality, or disrespect. Our society holds certain positive values dear and those values cannot, and should not, be compromised. However, when well-meaning people disagree and their essential values are not endangered, our democratic society depends on reasonable compromise.

(Nick Voges at nick@nmpolitics.net. See http://www.nmpolitics.net/index/2010/09/is-compromise-a-virtue/, *Is Compromise a Virtue?*)

John F. Kennedy addressed the issues of compromise in his book *Profiles in Courage*, when he wrote,

> *"We shall need compromise in the days ahead to be sure. But these will be, or should be, compromises of issues, not of principles. We can compromise our political positions, but not ourselves.... Compromise does not mean cowardice. Indeed it is frequently the compromisers and conciliators who are forced with the severest tests of political courage as they oppose the extremist views of their constituents"* Id.

President Eisenhower also credits the value of compromise when he said,

> *"Things are not all black and white. There have to be compromises. The middle of the road is all of the usable surface. The extremes, right and left, are in the gutters".*

The ability of people to solve problems within Servant Governing is enhanced, and actually facilitated, because the framework itself is not political or personality driven. Servant Governing is value-centered. It is neither conservative nor liberal. Tolerance for divergent beliefs within the framework stems from Servant Governing's singular focus on identifying, achieving and perpetuating the public good. Moreover, such tolerance is strengthened because public officials and public employees operating within a Servant Governing Framework believe they are "servants first". Being a "servant first" supersedes one's own political affiliation or ambition.

Political difference of opinion expressed in a civil manner is as American as apple pie. Such expressions of political differences help to define the common good through consensus building. However, rancorous argument and hateful ideological contentiousness do not further the achievement of the public good. Compromise on principle is not expected. Compromise on issues is often necessary for the public good to be achieved. Respect for both must always be maintained.

Unfortunately, over the last couple of decades we have allowed government to become needlessly limited in its problem-solving ability from within because of the uncharacteristic focus on our political differences, rather than a focus on the traditional American goal of reaching a consensus wherever possible for the common good of all. Servant Governing's Cornerstones of People, Principles, Priorities and Performance are a potent antidote to political intransigence, and are a cure for political malaise. Servant Governing promotes civility because it is performance-oriented and fact-based.

The bottom line is American government organizations can do better to solve problems on behalf of citizens. May Americans always use their God given abilities to reason and work together for the common good of all.

Servant Leadership and Health

One additional item I want to address concerns the issue of health and its importance to the servant leader. Everyone agrees that personal health is a necessary part of the leadership if the leader is to be effective. It takes stamina and strength of body to withstand the day-to-day stresses which a leader is subjected to in the course of organizational leadership. Nurturing and caring for others and their well-being in the organization by the leader may leave little time for attending to one's own personal health needs if the leader is not mindful of stress of leadership and its effects.

I speak from personal experience when I say a leader's health can deteriorate without much warning. I have always kept myself in reasonably good physical condition. However, two years ago in 2010, I noticed I was experiencing a great deal of fatigue in the early afternoon each day at work. I was enjoying my work immensely and it was gratifying to see the results of Servant Governing in action as the organization reached higher and higher levels of achievement and performance.

Finally, I reached the point of needing to call my doctor who told me to come over to see him. I am a believer in routine physicals, but I had not been as faithful as I should have been about them.

What the doctor discovered shocked me. He said I had elevated blood sugar. He admitted me to the hospital for one day for further tests. That night in the hospital around 2:00 a.m. I was awake and I felt I needed to pray to God to help me with my health I am a praying person, but not normally for myself.

I remember praying, "Lord, I could use some help with these blood sugar numbers." As soon as I finished uttering those words in my prayer, there was an immediate, strong sense inside me of the words, "If you are not fit, I can't use you." I did not actually hear the words, I felt them. It was an overwhelmingly powerful feeling. A little while later, I said the same prayer, and the same response was clear in my spirit, "If you're not fit, I can't use you." Well, that occurred three more times that night when, at last, I said, "Alright Lord. I get it. I'll do what I have to do with your help!"

The next day I was sent to an endocrinologist who told me I was going to be a candidate for insulin if I didn't get the blood sugar under control. The doctor gave me some pills and a book on carbohydrates and their affect on the body.

The following day I also visited the first doctor who admitted me to the hospital. When I walked into the room, the doctor gave me a prescription he had written. I looked at the piece of paper where the doctor had written, "The Perfect 10" by Dr. Aziz. The doctor said that the book by Dr. Aziz had changed the doctor's life and that's why he recommended it to me.

Of course, I went home and immediately downloaded Dr. Aziz's book on my Kindle®. As I read the book, I was astounded about how little I knew about my body and the affect stress was having on it. Over the course of the next several months, I totally changed my eating habits in accordance with Dr. Aziz's recommendations in the book. My wife, Sarah, and I began an exercise program which included walking a mile or more every day. I dropped forty pounds and my blood sugar levels went back to normal. My energy level returned and my health is excellent without insulin or pills. My wife's health improved as well since we approached the issue together. I thank God and my doctors for helping me to overcome my health setback.

Here is what I learned from Dr. Aziz's book. There are ten basic hormones in our bodies which need to be in balance for us to remain healthy. The stress of leadership can cause an imbalance of hormones, especially cortisol. Excessive cortisol can cause a reduction in insulin production, which results in weight gain and high blood sugar. If not corrected, this imbalance can lead to long-term adverse effects on the body which can limit the leader's ability to lead effectively.

The long and short of this discussion is that leadership is exhilarating, satisfying and rewarding. There is no greater reward than to serve one's fellow man. However, caution must be taken in the process of being a leader to take care of oneself in order to continue serving. "If you're not fit, I can't use you."

I am sure there are other books which could be just as helpful, but it is from personal experience that I know that the *Perfect 10* book gives the reader a great understanding of the relationship between health and hormonal balance. The servant leader would be well-advised to heed the advice. (See www.perfect10diet.com).

Thank you.
Ed Dean

BIBLIOGRAPHY

1. Active Strategy.
   http://www.activestrategy.com

2. Army.
   http://www.army.mil/values

3. Aziz, Michael, M.D. "The Perfect 10 Diet." 2010
   http://www.ThePerfect10Diet.com

4. Baron, Tony *The Art of Servant Leadership.* Wheatmark, 2013.

5. Boeing. http://www.boeing.com

6. Collins, Jim *Good to Great: Why Some Companies Make the Leap ... and Others Don't.* HarperCollins, 2001.

7. Community Tool Box. http://ctb.ku.edu

8. Covey, Dr. Stephen R. *The 4 Disciplines of Execution: Achieving Your Wildly Important Goals.* McChesney, Covey and Hurling, 2012

9. Florida Sterling Council. http://www.floridasterling.com

10. Franklin Covey. "Four Disciplines Execution." http://www.franklincovey.com/tc/solutions/business-execution-solutions/the-4-disciplines-of-execution-manager-certification/objectives

11. Robert K. Greenleaf Center for Servant Leadership, http://www.greenleaf.org

12. Greenleaf, R. *Servant Leadership,* Paulist Press, 1977.

13. "International Rankings of the United States." http://en.wikipedia.org/wiki/International rankings of the United States

14. Journal of Virtues and Leadership, Vol. 1, Iss. 1, 2010, 25-30; Regent University

15. Kennedy, John F. *Profiles in Courage*

16. Lockman Foundation. "New American Standard Bible®" copyright© 1960, 1962, 1963, 1968, 1971, 1972, 1973, 1975, 1977, 1995. http://www.lockman.org

17. Mokoto, Rich. "U.S. Students Still Lag Globally in Math and Science Tests Show." *New York Times* December 11, 2012.

18. Nagy, J., ed. Berkowitz and Schultz. *Servant Leadership: Accepting and Maintaining the Call of Service.*

19. North Carolina Department of Transportation.
    http://www.ncdot.gov

20. O'Donovan, Dana and Fowler, Noah *The Strategic Plan is Dead.* Stanford Social Innovation Review, Vol. 11, No. 2. Jan. 29, 2013

21. "Ranking America." Wood Press
    http://rankingamerica.wordpress.com/

22. Spears, L.C. *Tracing the Past, Present and Future of Servant Leadership.* In *Focus on Leadership: Servant Leadership for the Twenty-first Century.* John Waley and Sons, Inc., 2002.

23. Servant Leadership Institute http://www.servantleadershipinstitute.com Servant Leader Institute. *Video of Art Barter.* http://www.servantleadershipinstitute.com

24. What Really Happened.
    http://www.whatreallyhappened.com

25. Voges, Nick, "Is Compromise a Virtue?"
    http://www.nmpolitics.net/index/2010/09/is-compromise-a-virtue/

APPENDIX A

FLORIDA STERLING CRITERIA FOR PERFORMANCE EXCELLENCE (2013)

(Reprinted by Permission)

CRITERIA FOR PERFORMANCE EXCELLENCE:
Framework

The requirements of the Criteria for Performance Excellence are embodied in seven categories, as follows:

1. Leadership
2. Strategic Planning
3. Customer Focus
4. **Measurement, Analysis, and Knowledge Management**
5. Workforce Focus
6. Operations Focus
7. Results

The figure below provides the framework connecting and integrating the categories.

From top to bottom, the framework has the following basic elements.

ORGANIZATIONAL PROFILE
Your Organizational Profile (top of figure) sets the context for the way your organization operates. Your organization's environment, key working relationships, and strategic situation—including competitive environment, strategic challenges and advantages, and performance improvement system—serve as an overarching guide for your organizational performance management system.

PERFORMANCE SYSTEM
The performance system is composed of the seven Sterling categories that define your processes and the results you achieve.

Leadership (Category 1), Strategic Planning (Category 2), and Customer Focus (Category 3) represent the leadership triad. These categories are placed together to emphasize the importance of a leadership focus on strategy and customers. Senior leaders set your organizational direction and seek future opportunities for your organization.

Workforce Focus (Category 5), Operations Focus (Category 6), and Results (Category 7) represent the results triad. Your organization's workforce and key operational processes accomplish the work of the organization that yields your overall performance results.

All actions point toward Results—a composite of product and service and process outcomes, customer-focused outcomes, workforce-focused outcomes, leadership and governance outcomes, and financial and market outcomes.

The horizontal arrow in the center of the framework links the leadership triad to the results triad, a linkage critical to organizational success. Furthermore, the arrow indicates the central relationship between Leadership (Category 1) and Results (Category 7). The two-headed arrows indicate the importance of feedback in an effective performance management system.

SYSTEM FOUNDATION
Measurement, Analysis, and Knowledge Management (Category 4) are critical to the effective management of your organization and to a fact-based, knowledge-driven system for improving performance and competitiveness. Measurement, analysis, and knowledge management serve as a foundation for the performance management system.

CRITERIA STRUCTURE
The seven Criteria categories shown in the figure are subdivided into items and areas to address.

ITEMS
There are 17 process and results items, each focusing on a major requirement. Item titles and point values are given on page 2. The item format is shown on page 28.

AREAS TO ADDRESS
Items consist of one or more areas to address (areas). Organizations should address their responses to the specific requirements of these areas.

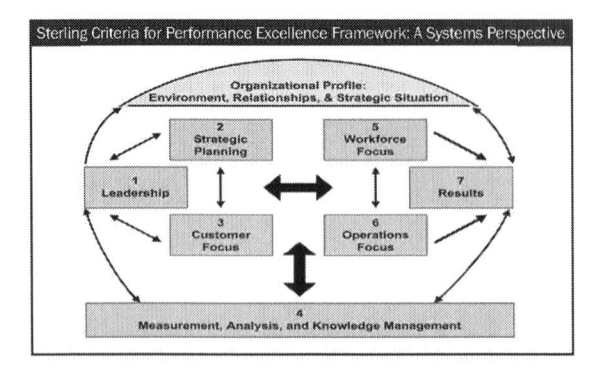

CRITERIA FOR PERFORMANCE EXCELLENCE:
Item List

P	**Preface: Organizational Profile**	
	P.1 Organizational Description	
	P.2 Organizational Situation	

Categories and Items — *Point Values*

1	**Leadership**	**140**
	1.1 Senior Leadership	80
	1.2 Governance and Societal Responsibility	60
2	**Strategic Planning**	**100**
	2.1 Strategy Development	50
	2.2 Strategy Implementation	50
3	**Customer Focus**	**100**
	3.1 Voice of the Customer	50
	3.2 Customer Engagement	50
4	**Measurement, Analysis, and Knowledge Management**	**100**
	4.1 Measurement, Analysis, and Improvement of Organizational Performance	50
	4.2 Management of Information, Knowledge, and Information Technology	50
5	**Workforce Focus**	**100**
	5.1 Workforce Environment	50
	5.2 Workforce Engagement	50
6	**Operations Focus**	**100**
	6.1 Work Systems	60
	6.2 Work Processes	40
7	**Results**	**360**
	7.1 Product and Service and Process Outcomes	110
	7.2 Customer-Focused Outcomes	70
	7.3 Workforce-Focused Outcomes	60
	7.4 Leadership and Governance Outcomes	60
	7.5 Financial and Market Outcomes	60
	TOTAL POINTS	**1,000**

Note: The Scoring system used with the Criteria items in a Sterling assessment can be found on pages 57-59.

CRITERIA FOR PERFORMANCE EXCELLENCE

The Importance of Beginning with Your Organizational Profile

Your Organizational Profile is critically important because:

- it is the most appropriate starting point for self-assessment and for writing an application;
- it helps you identify potential gaps in key information and focus on key performance requirements and results;
- it is used by the examiners and judges in application review, including the site visit, to understand your organization and what you consider important (you will be assessed using the Criteria requirements in relation to your organization's environment, relationships, influences, and challenges, as presented in your Organizational Profile); and
- it also may be used by itself for an initial self-assessment.

P   Preface: Organizational Profile

The *Organizational Profile* is a snapshot of your organization, the KEY influences on HOW you operate, and the KEY challenges you face. For definitions of key terms presented throughout the Criteria and scoring guidelines text in SMALL CAPS, see the Glossary of Key Terms on pages 49-56.

P.1 Organizational Description: What are your key organizational characteristics?

Describe your organization's operating environment and your KEY relationships with CUSTOMERS, suppliers, PARTNERS, and STAKEHOLDERS.

Within your response, include answers to the following questions:

a. **Organizational Environment**

   (1) **Product and Service Offerings** What are your organization's main product and service offerings (see note 1 below)? What is the relative importance of each to your organizational success? What mechanisms do you use to deliver your products and services?

   (2) **Vision and Mission** What are the distinctive characteristics of your organizational culture? What are your stated PURPOSE, VISION, VALUES, and MISSION? What are your organization's CORE COMPETENCIES and their relationship to your MISSION?

   (3) **Workforce Profile** What is your WORKFORCE profile? What are your WORKFORCE or employee groups and SEGMENTS? What are their education levels? What are the KEY elements that engage them in accomplishing your MISSION and VISION? What are your organization's WORKFORCE and job DIVERSITY, organized bargaining units, KEY WORKFORCE benefits, and special health and safety requirements?

   (4) **Assets** What are your major facilities, technologies, and equipment?

   (5) **Regulatory Requirements** What is the regulatory environment under which your organization operates? What are the applicable occupational health and safety regulations; accreditation, certification, or registration requirements; industry standards; and environmental, financial, and product and service regulations?

b. **Organizational Relationships**

   (1) **Organizational Structure** What are your organizational structure and GOVERNANCE system? What are the reporting relationships among your GOVERNANCE board, SENIOR LEADERS, and parent organization, as appropriate?

   (2) **Customers and Stakeholders** What are your KEY market SEGMENTS, CUSTOMER groups, and STAKEHOLDER groups, as appropriate? What are their KEY requirements and expectations for your products and services, CUSTOMER support services, and operations? What are the differences in these requirements and expectations among market SEGMENTS, CUSTOMER groups, and STAKEHOLDER groups?

   (3) **Suppliers and Partners** What are your KEY types of suppliers, PARTNERS, and COLLABORATORS? What role do these suppliers, PARTNERS, and COLLABORATORS play in the production and delivery of your KEY products and services and CUSTOMER support services? What are your KEY mechanisms for communicating with suppliers, PARTNERS, and COLLABORATORS? What role, if any, do these organizations play in implementing INNOVATIONS in your organization? What are your KEY supply-chain requirements?

Notes:

N1. "Product and service offerings" and "products and services" (P.1a[1]) refer to the goods and services that your organization offers in the marketplace. Mechanisms for product and service delivery to your end-use customers might be direct or through dealers, distributors, collaborators, or channel partners. *Nonprofit organizations might refer to their product and service offerings as programs, projects, or services.*

N2. "Core competencies" (P.1a[2]) refers to your organization's areas of greatest expertise. Your organization's core competencies are those strategically important capabilities that are central to fulfilling your mission or provide an advantage in your marketplace or service environment. Core competencies frequently are challenging for competitors or suppliers and partners to imitate. Also, core competencies frequently preserve your competitive advantage.

N3. Workforce or employee groups and segments (including organized bargaining units; P.1a[3]) might be based on the type of employment or contract reporting relationship, location, tour of duty, work environment, family-friendly policies, or other factors.

N4. Customer groups (P.1b[2]) might be based on common expectations, behaviors, preferences, or profiles. Within a group there may be customer segments based on differences and commonalities. Your markets might be subdivided into market segments based on product lines or features, distribution channels, business volume, geography, or other factors that your organization uses to define related market characteristics.

N5. Customer group and market segment requirements (P.1b[2]) might include on-time delivery, low defect levels, safety, security, ongoing price reductions, leveraging of technology, rapid response, after-sales service, and multilingual services. Stakeholder group requirements might include socially responsible behavior and community service. *For some nonprofit organizations, requirements also might include administrative cost reductions, at-home services, and rapid response to emergencies.*

N6. Communication mechanisms (P.1b[3]) should be two-way and in understandable language, and they might be in person, via e-mail, Web-based, or by telephone. For many organizations, these mechanisms may change as marketplace, customer, or stakeholder requirements change.

N7. Many nonprofit organizations rely heavily on volunteers to accomplish their work. These organizations should include volunteers in the discussion of their workforce (P.1a[3]).

N8. For nonprofit organizations, industry standards (P.1a[5]) might include industry-wide codes of conduct and policy guidance. The term "industry" is used throughout the Criteria to refer to the sector in which you operate. For nonprofit organizations, this sector might be charitable organizations, professional associations and societies, religious organizations, or government entities—or a subsector of one of these.

N9. For some nonprofit organizations, governance and reporting relationships (P.1b[1]) might include relationships with major agency, foundation, or other funding sources.

N10. Customers (P.1b[2]) include the users and potential users of your products and services. In some nonprofit organizations, customers might include members, taxpayers, citizens, recipients, clients, and beneficiaries. Market segments might be referred to as constituencies.

For additional description of this item, see pages 32-33.

INFORMATION FOR UNDERSTANDING ALL CRITERIA ITEMS

- For definitions of key terms presented throughout the Criteria and scoring guidelines text in SMALL CAPS, see the Glossary of Key Terms on pages 49-56.
- Frequently, several questions are grouped under one number (e.g., P.1a[3]). These questions are related and do not require separate responses. These multiple questions serve as a guide in understanding the full meaning of the information being requested.
- The items in the Sterling Criteria are divided into three groups: the Preface, which defines your organizational environment; Categories 1–6, which define your organization's processes; and Category 7, which contains your results for your organization's processes. Only responses to the last two groups are scored during a Sterling Award evaluation of an organization; the Organizational Profile items are used to provide context for the evaluation.
- Item notes serve three purposes: (1) to clarify terms or requirements presented in an item, (2) to give instructions and examples for responding to the item requirements, and (3) to indicate key linkages to other items. In all cases, the intent is to help you respond to the item requirements.
- A number of item notes include guidance specifically for nonprofit organizations. This information appears in italics.

Additional Health Care and Education notes can be downloaded from our website at www.floridasterling.com under the *Governor's Sterling Award* tab.

P.2 Organizational Situation: What is your organization's strategic situation?

Describe your organization's competitive environment, your KEY STRATEGIC CHALLENGES and ADVANTAGES, and your system for PERFORMANCE improvement.

Within your response, include answers to the following questions:

a. **Competitive Environment**
   (1) **Competitive Position** What is your competitive position? What are your relative size and growth in your industry or markets served? What are the numbers and types of competitors for your organization?
   (2) **Competitiveness Changes** What are any KEY changes taking place that affect your competitive situation, including opportunities for INNOVATION and collaboration, as appropriate?
   (3) **Comparative Data** What are your KEY available sources of comparative and competitive data from within your industry? What are your KEY available sources of comparative data from outside your industry? What limitations, if any, affect your ability to obtain these data?

b. **Strategic Context**
   What are your KEY business, operational, societal responsibility, and human resource STRATEGIC CHALLENGES and ADVANTAGES?

c. **PERFORMANCE Improvement System**
   What are the KEY elements of your PERFORMANCE improvement system, including your evaluation, organizational LEARNING, and INNOVATION PROCESSES?

Notes:

N1. Strategic challenges and advantages (P.2b) might relate to technology, products and services, your operations, your customer support, your industry, globalization, your value chain, and people. Strategic advantages might include differentiators such as your price, leadership, design services, innovation rate, geographic proximity, accessibility, and warranty and product and service options. *For some nonprofit organizations, differentiators also might include your relative influence with decision makers, ratio of administrative costs to programmatic contributions, reputation for program or service delivery, and wait times for service.*

N2. Performance improvement (P.2c) through learning and integration is an assessment dimension used in the scoring system to evaluate the maturity of organizational approaches and deployment (see pages 57-59). This question is intended to help you and the Sterling examiners set an overall context for your approach to performance improvement. Approaches to performance improvement that are compatible with the systems approach provided by the Sterling framework should be related to your organization's needs and might include implementing a Lean Enterprise System, applying Six Sigma methodology, using ISO standards (e.g., 9000 or 14000), or employing other process improvement and innovation tools. A growing number of organizations have implemented specific processes for meeting goals in product and service and process innovation.

N3. *Nonprofit organizations frequently are in a highly competitive environment; they often must compete with other organizations and with alternative sources for similar services to secure financial and volunteer resources, membership, visibility in appropriate communities, and media attention.*

N4. *For nonprofit organizations, the term "business" (P.2b) is used throughout the Criteria to refer to your main mission area or enterprise activity.*

For additional description of this item, see pages 32-33.

Page Limit
For Sterling Award applicants, the Organizational Profile is limited to five pages. These pages are not counted in the overall application page limit. Typing and formatting instructions for the Organizational Profile are the same as for the application. These instructions are given in the Sterling Award Application Forms, which can be downloaded at www.floridasterling.com.

EXAMINATION CRITERIA

1 Leadership (140 pts.)

The Leadership category examines HOW your organization's SENIOR LEADERS' personal actions guide and sustain your organization. Also examined are your organization's GOVERNANCE system and HOW your organization fulfills its legal, ethical, and societal responsibilities and supports its KEY communities.

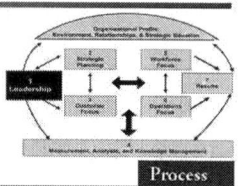

1.1 Senior Leadership: How do your senior leaders lead? (80 pts.)   Process

Describe HOW SENIOR LEADERS' actions guide and sustain your organization. Describe HOW SENIOR LEADERS communicate with your WORKFORCE and encourage HIGH PERFORMANCE.

Within your response, include answers to the following questions:

a. VISION, VALUES, and MISSION

   (1) **Vision and Values** HOW do SENIOR LEADERS set your organization's VISION and VALUES? HOW do SENIOR LEADERS DEPLOY your organization's VISION and VALUES through your LEADERSHIP SYSTEM, to the WORKFORCE, to KEY suppliers and PARTNERS, and to CUSTOMERS and other STAKEHOLDERS, as appropriate? HOW do SENIOR LEADERS' actions reflect a commitment to the organization's VALUES?

   (2) **Promoting Legal and Ethical Behavior** HOW do SENIOR LEADERS' actions demonstrate their commitment to legal and ETHICAL BEHAVIOR? HOW do they promote an organizational environment that requires it?

   (3) **Creating a Sustainable Organization** HOW do SENIOR LEADERS create a SUSTAINABLE organization? HOW do SENIOR LEADERS achieve the following?

   - create an environment for organizational PERFORMANCE improvement, the accomplishment of your MISSION and STRATEGIC OBJECTIVES, INNOVATION, PERFORMANCE leadership, and organizational agility
   - create a WORKFORCE culture that delivers a consistently positive CUSTOMER experience and fosters CUSTOMER ENGAGEMENT
   - create an environment for organizational and WORKFORCE LEARNING
   - develop and enhance their leadership skills
   - participate in organizational LEARNING, succession planning, and the development of future organizational leaders

b. Communication and Organizational PERFORMANCE

   (1) **Communication** HOW do SENIOR LEADERS communicate with and engage the entire WORKFORCE? HOW do SENIOR LEADERS achieve the following?

   - encourage frank, two-way communication throughout the organization
   - communicate KEY decisions
   - Take an active role in reward and recognition programs to reinforce HIGH PERFORMANCE and a CUSTOMER and business focus

   (2) **Focus on Action** HOW do SENIOR LEADERS create a focus on action to accomplish the organization's objectives, improve PERFORMANCE, and attain its VISION? HOW do SENIOR LEADERS identify needed actions? HOW do SENIOR LEADERS include a focus on creating and balancing VALUE for CUSTOMERS and other STAKEHOLDERS in their organizational PERFORMANCE expectations?

Notes:

N1. Organizational vision (1.1a[1]) should set the context for strategic objectives and action plans, which are described in Items 2.1 and 2.2.

N2. A sustainable organization (1.1a[3]) is capable of addressing current business needs and possesses the agility and strategic management to prepare successfully for its future business, market, and operating environment. Both external and internal factors are considered. In this context, the concept of innovation includes both technological and organizational innovation to help the organization succeed in the future. A sustainable organization also ensures a safe and secure environment for the workforce and other key stakeholders. An organization's contributions to environmental, social, and economic systems beyond those of its workforce and immediate stakeholders are considered in its societal responsibilities (Item 1.2).

N3. A focus on action (1.1b[2]) considers the strategy, the workforce, the work systems, and the assets of your organization. It includes taking intelligent risks and implementing innovations and ongoing improvements in productivity that may be achieved through eliminating waste or reducing cycle time; it might use techniques such as Six Sigma and Lean. It also includes the actions to accomplish your organization's strategic objectives (see 2.2a[1]).

N4. Your organizational performance results should be reported in Items 7.1–7.5.

N5. *For nonprofit organizations that rely on volunteers to accomplish their work, responses to 1.1b(1) also should discuss your efforts to communicate with and engage the volunteer workforce.*

For additional description of this item, see page 33.

1.2 **Governance and Societal Responsibilities:** How do you govern and fulfill
your societal responsibilities? (60 pts.)

Process

Describe your organization's **GOVERNANCE** system and **APPROACH** to leadership improvement. Describe **HOW** your organization ensures legal and **ETHICAL BEHAVIOR**, fulfills its societal responsibilities, and supports its **KEY** communities.

Within your response, include answers to the following questions:

a. **Organizational GOVERNANCE**

(1) **Governance System** **HOW** does your organization review and achieve the following **KEY** aspects of your **GOVERNANCE** system:
- accountability for management's actions
- fiscal accountability
- transparency in operations and selection of and disclosure policies for **GOVERNANCE** board members, as appropriate
- independence in internal and external audits
- protection of **STAKEHOLDER** and stockholder interests, as appropriate

(2) **Performance Evaluation** **HOW** do you evaluate the **PERFORMANCE** of your **SENIOR LEADERS**, including the chief executive? **HOW** do you use these **PERFORMANCE** evaluations in determining executive compensation? **HOW** do you evaluate the **PERFORMANCE** of members of your **GOVERNANCE** board, as appropriate? **HOW** do **SENIOR LEADERS** and your **GOVERNANCE** board use these **PERFORMANCE** reviews to advance their development and improve both their personal leadership **EFFECTIVENESS** and that of your board and **LEADERSHIP SYSTEM**, as appropriate?

b. **Legal and ETHICAL BEHAVIOR**

(1) **Legal and Regulatory Behavior** **HOW** do you address any adverse impacts on society of your products and services and operations? **HOW** do you anticipate public concerns with current and future products and services and operations? **HOW** do you prepare for these impacts and concerns in a proactive manner, including conserving natural resources and using **EFFECTIVE** supply-chain management **PROCESSES**, as appropriate? What are your **KEY** compliance **PROCESSES**, **MEASURES**, and **GOALS** for achieving and surpassing regulatory and legal requirements, as appropriate? What are your **KEY PROCESSES, MEASURES**, and **GOALS** for addressing risks associated with your products and services and operations?

(2) **Ethical Behavior** **HOW** does your organization promote and ensure **ETHICAL BEHAVIOR** in all interactions? What are your **KEY PROCESSES** and **MEASURES** or **INDICATORS** for enabling and monitoring **ETHICAL BEHAVIOR** in your **GOVERNANCE** structure, throughout your organization, and in interactions with **CUSTOMERS, PARTNERS**, suppliers, and other **STAKEHOLDERS**? **HOW** do you monitor and respond to breaches of **ETHICAL BEHAVIOR**?

c. **Societal Responsibilities and Support of KEY Communities**

(1) **Societal Well-Being** **HOW** do you consider societal well-being and benefit as part of your strategy and daily operations? **HOW** do you contribute to the well-being of your environmental, social, and economic systems?

(2) **Community Support** **HOW** does your organization actively support and strengthen your **KEY** communities? What are your **KEY** communities? **HOW** do you identify these communities and determine areas for organizational involvement, including areas related to your **CORE COMPETENCIES**? **HOW** do your **SENIOR LEADERS**, in concert with your **WORKFORCE**, contribute to improving these communities?

Notes:

N1. Societal responsibilities in areas critical to your organization's ongoing marketplace success also should be addressed in Strategy Development (Item 2.1) and in Operations Focus (Category 6). Key results, such as results related to regulatory and legal requirements (including the results of mandated financial audits); reductions in environmental impacts through the use of "green" technology, resource-conserving activities, or other means; or improvements in social impacts, such as the global use of enlightened labor practices, should be reported as Leadership and Governance Outcomes (Item 7.4).

N2. Transparency in operations of your governance system (1.2a[1]) should include your internal controls on governance processes. *For some nonprofit organizations, an external advisory board may provide some or all of the governance board functions. For those nonprofit organizations that serve as stewards of public funds, stewardship of those funds and transparency in operations are areas of emphasis.*

N3. Leadership performance evaluation (1.2a[2]) might be supported by peer reviews, formal performance management reviews, and formal or informal workforce and other stakeholder feedback and surveys. *For some nonprofit and government organizations, external advisory boards might evaluate the performance of senior leaders and the governance board.*

N4. Measures or indicators of ethical behavior (1.2b[2]) might include the percentage of independent board members, measures of relationships with stockholder and nonstockholder constituencies, instances of ethical conduct breaches and responses, survey results on workforce perceptions of organizational ethics, ethics hotline use, and results of ethics reviews and audits. They also might include evidence that policies, workforce training, and monitoring systems are in place with respect to conflicts of interest and proper use of funds.

1.2 (continued)

N5. Areas of societal contributions and community support appropriate for 1.2c might include your efforts to improve the environment (e.g., collaboration to conserve the environment or natural resources); strengthen local community services, education, and health; and improve the practices of trade, business, or professional associations.

N6. The health and safety of your workforce are not addressed in Item 1.2; you should address these workforce factors in Item 5.1.

N7. *Nonprofit organizations should report in 1.2b(1), as appropriate, how they address the legal and regulatory requirements and standards that govern fundraising and lobbying activities.*

N8. *For some charitable organizations, societal contributions and support of key communities (1.2c) may occur totally through the mission-related activities of the organization. In such cases, it is appropriate to respond with any "extra efforts" through which you support these communities.*

For additional description of this item, see pages 33-34.

Assessment of Item Responses
Item responses are assessed by considering the Criteria item requirements; your key business factors presented in your Organizational Profile; and the maturity of your approaches, breadth of their deployment, and strength of your improvement process and results relative to the scoring system. Refer to the scoring system information on pages 57-59.

"We began our journey in 1997 with leadership's commitment to continuous improvement and performance excellence. The Sterling/Malcolm Baldrige Criteria provides the framework for our management system and helped us to define our mission, vision, values, and strategic priorities. As a result, we have transitioned from a reactive to proactive high performing culture that is data-driven and embraces its internal and external customer groups. The Criteria have enabled us to sustain our direction, measure and improve how service is delivered to our customers, and develop and strengthen collaborative community partnerships that have resulted in positive trends from critical health outcomes."

- Lillian Rivera, Administrator, Miami-Dade County Health Department
2002 and 2006 Governor's Sterling Award Recipient

2 Strategic Planning (100 pts.)

The *Strategic Planning* Category examines **HOW** your organization develops **STRATEGIC OBJECTIVES** and **ACTION PLANS**. Also examined are **HOW** your chosen **STRATEGIC OBJECTIVES** and **ACTION PLANS** are **DEPLOYED** and changed if circumstances require, and **HOW** progress is measured.

2.1 Strategy Development: How do you develop your strategy? (50 pts.)

Process

Describe **HOW** your organization establishes its strategy to address its **STRATEGIC CHALLENGES** and leverage its **STRATEGIC ADVANTAGES**. Summarize your organization's **KEY STRATEGIC OBJECTIVES** and their related **GOALS**.

Within your response, include answers to the following questions:

a. Strategy Development PROCESS

(1) **Strategic Planning Process** HOW does your organization conduct its strategic planning? What are the **KEY PROCESS** steps? Who are the **KEY** participants? **HOW** does your **PROCESS** identify potential blind spots? **HOW** do you determine your **CORE COMPETENCIES**, **STRATEGIC CHALLENGES**, and **STRATEGIC ADVANTAGES** (identified in your Organizational Profile)? What are your short- and longer-term planning time horizons? **HOW** are these time horizons set? **HOW** does your strategic planning **PROCESS** address these time horizons?

(2) **Strategic Considerations** HOW do you ensure that strategic planning addresses the **KEY** factors listed below? **HOW** do you collect and analyze relevant data and information pertaining to these factors as part of your strategic planning **PROCESS**?
- your organization's strengths, weaknesses, opportunities, and threats
- early indications of major shifts in technology, markets, products and services, **CUSTOMER** preferences, competition, the economy, and the regulatory environment
- long-term organizational **SUSTAINABILITY**, including needed **CORE COMPETENCIES**, and **PROJECTIONS** of your future **PERFORMANCE** and your competitors' or comparable organizations' future **PERFORMANCE**
- your ability to execute the strategic plan

b. STRATEGIC OBJECTIVES

(1) **Key Strategic Objectives** What are your **KEY STRATEGIC OBJECTIVES** and your timetable for accomplishing them? What are your most important **GOALS** for these **STRATEGIC OBJECTIVES**?

(2) **Strategic Objective Considerations** HOW do your **STRATEGIC OBJECTIVES** achieve the following?
- address your **STRATEGIC CHALLENGES** and **STRATEGIC ADVANTAGES**
- address your opportunities for **INNOVATION** in products and services, operations, and your business model
- capitalize on your current **CORE COMPETENCIES** and address the potential need for new **CORE COMPETENCIES**
- balance short- and longer-term challenges and opportunities
- consider and balance the needs of all **KEY STAKEHOLDERS**
- enhance your ability to adapt to sudden shifts in your market conditions

Notes:

N1. "Strategy development" refers to your organization's approach to preparing for the future. Strategy development might utilize various types of forecasts, projections, options, scenarios, knowledge (see 4.2a for relevant organizational knowledge), or other approaches to envisioning the future for purposes of decision making and resource allocation. Strategy development might involve participation by key suppliers, distributors, partners, and customers. *For some nonprofit organizations, strategy development might involve participation by organizations providing similar services or drawing from the same donor population or volunteer workforce.*

N2. The term "strategy" should be interpreted broadly. Strategy might be built around or lead to any or all of the following: new products and services; redefinition of key customer groups or market segments; intelligent risks; new core competencies; revenue growth via various approaches, including acquisitions, grants, and endowments; divestitures; new partnerships and alliances; and new employee or volunteer relationships. Strategy might be directed toward becoming a preferred supplier, a local supplier in each of your major customers' or partners' markets, a low-cost producer, a market innovator, or a provider of a high-end or customized product or service. It also might be directed toward meeting a community or public need.

N3. Your organization's strengths, weaknesses, opportunities, and threats (2.1a[2]) should address all factors that are key to your organization's future success, including the following, as appropriate: your customer and market requirements, expectations, and opportunities; your opportunities for innovation and role-model performance; your core competencies; your competitive environment and your performance now and in the future relative to competitors and comparable organizations; your product and service life cycle; technological and other key innovations or changes that might affect your products and services and how you operate, as well as the rate of innovation; your workforce and other resource needs; your ability to capitalize on diversity; your opportunities to redirect resources to higher-priority products, services, or areas; financial, societal, ethical, regulatory, technological, security, and other potential risks and opportunities; your ability to prevent and respond to emergencies, including natural or other disasters; changes in the national or global economy; requirements for and strengths and weaknesses of your partners and supply chain; changes in your parent organization; and other factors unique to your organization.

N4. Your ability to execute the strategic plan (2.1a[2]) should address your ability to mobilize the necessary resources and knowledge. It also should address your organizational agility based on contingency plans or, if circumstances require, a shift in plans and rapid execution of new or changed plans.

N5. Strategic objectives that address key challenges and advantages (2.1b[2]) might include rapid response, customization, co-location with major customers or partners, workforce capability and capacity, specific joint ventures, virtual manufacturing, rapid innovation, ISO quality or environmental systems registration, societal responsibility actions or leadership, Web-based supplier and customer relationship management, and product and service quality enhancements. Responses to Item 2.1 should focus on your specific challenges and advantages—those most important to your ongoing success and to strengthening your organization's overall performance.

N6. Item 2.1 addresses your overall organizational strategy, which might include changes in product and service offerings and customer engagement processes. However, the item does not address product and service design or customer engagement strategies; you should address these factors in Items 3.2 and 6.1, as appropriate.

For additional description of this item, see pages 34-35.

"The Governor's Sterling Award validates our commitment to continuously strive for a higher level of quality compassionate care. Our journey taught us the value of all being on the same page, focusing on the same goals, and striving for the highest level of excellence."

- Lincoln Mendez, CEO, South Miami Hospital
Javier Hernandez-Lichtl, Former CEO, South Miami Hospital
2010 Governor's Sterling Award Recipient

"The Sterling management system helped The Ritz-Carlton, Sarasota improve the execution of our strategy, enhance workforce engagement, and demonstrate sustained customer loyalty and business results."

- Jim McManemon, General Manager, The Ritz-Carlton, Sarasota
2008 Governor's Sterling Award Recipient

2.2 Strategy Implementation: How do you implement your strategy? (50 pts.)

Process

Describe HOW your organization converts its STRATEGIC OBJECTIVES into ACTION PLANS. Summarize your organization's ACTION PLANS, HOW they are DEPLOYED, and KEY ACTION PLAN PERFORMANCE MEASURES or INDICATORS. Project your organization's future PERFORMANCE relative to KEY comparisons on these PERFORMANCE MEASURES or INDICATORS.

Within your response, include answers to the following questions:

a. ACTION PLAN Development and DEPLOYMENT

(1) **Action Plan Development** HOW do you develop your ACTION PLANS? What are your KEY short- and longer-term ACTION PLANS and their relationship to your STRATEGIC OBJECTIVES? What are the KEY planned changes, if any, in your products and services, your CUSTOMERS and markets, your suppliers and PARTNERS, and how you will operate?

(2) **Action Plan Implementation** HOW do you DEPLOY ACTION PLANS throughout the organization to your WORKFORCE and to KEY suppliers and PARTNERS, as appropriate, to achieve your KEY STRATEGIC OBJECTIVES? HOW do you ensure that the KEY outcomes of your ACTION PLANS can be sustained?

(3) **Resource Allocation** HOW do you ensure that financial and other resources are available to support the accomplishment of your ACTION PLANS, while meeting current obligations? HOW do you allocate these resources to support the accomplishment of the plans? HOW do you manage the financial and other risks associated with the plans to ensure the financial viability of your organization?

(4) **Workforce Plans** What are your KEY human resource or WORKFORCE plans to accomplish your short- and longer-term STRATEGIC OBJECTIVES and ACTION PLANS? HOW do the plans address potential impacts on your WORKFORCE members and any potential changes to WORKFORCE CAPABILITY and CAPACITY needs?

(5) **Performance Measures** What are your KEY PERFORMANCE MEASURES or INDICATORS for tracking the achievement and EFFECTIVENESS of your ACTION PLANS? HOW do you ensure that your overall ACTION PLAN measurement system reinforces organizational ALIGNMENT? HOW do you ensure that the measurement system covers all KEY DEPLOYMENT areas and STAKEHOLDERS?

(6) **Action Plan Modification** HOW do you establish and implement modified ACTION PLANS if circumstances require a shift in plans and rapid execution of new plans?

b. PERFORMANCE PROJECTION

For the KEY PERFORMANCE MEASURES or INDICATORS identified in 2.2a(5), what are your PERFORMANCE PROJECTIONS for both your short- and longer-term planning time horizons? HOW does your projected PERFORMANCE on these measures or INDICATORS compare with the projected PERFORMANCE of your competitors or comparable organizations? How does it compare with KEY BENCHMARKS, GOALS, and past PERFORMANCE, as appropriate? If there are current or projected gaps in PERFORMANCE against your competitors or comparable organizations, HOW will you address them?

Notes:

N1. Strategy and action plan development and deployment are closely linked to other items in the Criteria. The following are examples of key linkages:

- Item 1.1 for how your senior leaders set and communicate organizational direction

- Category 3 for gathering customer and market knowledge as input to your strategy and action plans and for deploying action plans

- Category 4 for measurement, analysis, and knowledge management to support your key information needs, support your development of strategy, provide an effective basis for your performance measurements, and track progress relative to your strategic objectives and action plans

- Category 5 for meeting your workforce capability and capacity needs, for workforce development and learning system design and needs, and for implementing workforce-related changes resulting from action plans

- Category 6 for changes to core competencies, work systems, and work process requirements resulting from your action plans

- Item 7.1 for specific accomplishments relative to your organizational strategy and action plans

N2. Measures and indicators of projected performance (2.2b) might include changes resulting from new ventures; organizational acquisitions or mergers; new value creation; market entry and shifts; new legislative mandates, legal requirements, or industry standards; and significant anticipated innovations in products and services and technology.

For additional description of this item, see pages 35-36.

3 Customer Focus (100 pts.)

The *Customer Focus* category examines HOW your organization engages its CUSTOMERS for long-term marketplace success. This ENGAGEMENT strategy includes HOW your organization listens to the VOICE OF ITS CUSTOMERS, builds CUSTOMER relationships, and uses CUSTOMER information to improve and identify opportunities for INNOVATION.

3.1 Voice of the Customer: How do you obtain information from your customers? (50 pts.) — Process

Describe HOW your organization listens to your CUSTOMERS and gains satisfaction and dissatisfaction information.

Within your response, include answers to the following questions:

a. CUSTOMER Listening

   (1) **Listening to Current Customers** HOW do you listen to CUSTOMERS to obtain actionable information? HOW do your listening methods vary for different CUSTOMERS, CUSTOMER groups, or market SEGMENTS? HOW do you use social media and Web-based technologies to listen to CUSTOMERS, as appropriate? HOW do your listening methods vary across the CUSTOMER life cycle? HOW do you follow up with CUSTOMERS on the quality of products and services, CUSTOMER support, and transactions to receive immediate and actionable feedback?

   (2) **Listening to Potential Customers** HOW do you listen to former CUSTOMERS, potential CUSTOMERS, and CUSTOMERS of competitors to obtain actionable information and to obtain feedback on your products and services, CUSTOMER support, and transactions, as appropriate?

b. Determination of CUSTOMER Satisfaction and ENGAGEMENT

   (1) **Satisfaction and Engagement** HOW do you determine CUSTOMER satisfaction and ENGAGEMENT? HOW do these determination methods differ among CUSTOMER groups and market SEGMENTS, as appropriate? HOW do your measurements capture actionable information for use in exceeding your CUSTOMERS' expectations and securing your CUSTOMERS' ENGAGEMENT?

   (2) **Satisfaction Relative to Competitors** HOW do you obtain information on your CUSTOMERS' satisfaction relative to their satisfaction with your competitors? HOW do you obtain information on your CUSTOMERS' satisfaction relative to the satisfaction LEVELS of CUSTOMERS of other organizations providing similar PRODUCTS AND SERVICES or to industry BENCHMARKS, as appropriate?

   (3) **Dissatisfaction** HOW do you determine CUSTOMER dissatisfaction? HOW do your measurements capture actionable information for use in meeting your CUSTOMERS' requirements and exceeding their expectations in the future?

Notes:

N1. The "voice of the customer" refers to your process for capturing customer-related information. Voice-of-the-customer processes are intended to be proactive and continuously innovative to capture stated, unstated, and anticipated customer requirements, expectations, and desires. The goal is to achieve customer engagement. Listening to the voice of the customer might include gathering and integrating various types of customer data, such as survey data, focus group findings, blog comments and other social media data, warranty data, marketing and sales information, and complaint data that affect customers' purchasing and engagement decisions.

N2. Use of social media and Web-based technologies to listen to customers (3.1a[1]) provides a newer mode of gathering insight into customer perceptions of all aspects of your involvement with them. Use of social media may include blogs moderated by your organization and unsolicited opportunities to learn based on social media outlets your organization does not control, such as wikis, online forums, and blogs not moderated by your organization.

N3. The customer life cycle (3.1a[1]) begins in the product and service concept or pre-sale period and should include all stages of your involvement with the customer. This might include relationship building, the active business relationship, and an exit strategy, as appropriate.

N4. Determining customer satisfaction and dissatisfaction (3.1b) might include the use of any or all of the following: surveys, formal and informal feedback, customer account histories, complaints, field reports, win/loss analysis, customer referral rates, and transaction completion rates. Information might be gathered on the Web, through personal contact or a third party, or by mail. Determining customer dissatisfaction should be seen as more than reviewing low customer satisfaction scores. Dissatisfaction should be independently deter-mined to identify root causes and enable a systematic remedy to avoid future dissatisfaction.

N5. Determining relative customer satisfaction (3.1b[2]) may involve comparisons with competitors, comparisons with other organizations that deliver similar products and services in a noncompetitive marketplace, or comparisons achieved through trade or other organizations. Determining relative customer satisfaction also may involve determining why customers chose your competitors over you.

N6. For *additional considerations on products and services and the business of nonprofit organizations, see Item P.1, Note 1, and Item P.2, Note 4*.

For additional description of this item, see page 36.

3.2 Customer Engagement: How do you engage customers to serve their needs and build relationships? (50 pts.)   **Process**

Describe HOW your organization determines product and service offerings and communication mechanisms to support CUSTOMERS. Describe HOW your organization builds CUSTOMER relationships.

Within your response, include answers to the following questions:

a. **Product and Service Offerings and CUSTOMER Support**

  (1) **Product and Service Offerings** HOW do you identify CUSTOMER and market requirements for product and offerings? HOW do you identify and innovate product and service offerings to meet the requirements and exceed the expectations of your CUSTOMER groups and market SEGMENTS (identified in your Organizational Profile)? HOW do you identify and innovate product and service offerings to enter new markets, to attract new CUSTOMERS, and to provide opportunities for expanding relationships with existing CUSTOMERS, as appropriate?

  (2) **Customer Support** HOW do you enable CUSTOMERS to seek information and CUSTOMER support? HOW do you enable them to conduct their business with you and provide feedback on your products and services and your CUSTOMER support? What are your KEY means of CUSTOMER support, including your KEY communication mechanisms? HOW do they vary for different CUSTOMERS, CUSTOMER groups, or market SEGMENTS? HOW do you determine your CUSTOMERS' KEY support requirements? HOW do you ensure that CUSTOMER support requirements are DEPLOYED to all people and PROCESSES involved in CUSTOMER support?

  (3) **Customer Segmentation** HOW do you use CUSTOMER, market, and product and service offering information to identify current and anticipate future CUSTOMER groups and market SEGMENTS? HOW do you consider CUSTOMERS of competitors and other potential CUSTOMERS and markets in this segmentation? HOW do you determine which CUSTOMERS, CUSTOMER groups, and market SEGMENTS to pursue for current and future products and services?

  (4) **Customer Data Use** HOW do you use CUSTOMER, market, and product and service offering information to improve marketing, build a more CUSTOMER-focused culture, and identify opportunities for INNOVATION?

b. **Building CUSTOMER Relationships**

  (1) **Relationship Management** HOW do you market, build, and manage relationships with CUSTOMERS to achieve the following?
   • acquire CUSTOMERS and build market share
   • retain CUSTOMERS, meet their requirements, and exceed their expectations in each stage of the CUSTOMER life cycle
   • increase their ENGAGEMENT with you

  (2) **Complaint Management** HOW do you manage CUSTOMER complaints? HOW does your CUSTOMER complaint management PROCESS ensure that complaints are resolved promptly and EFFECTIVELY? HOW does your CUSTOMER complaint management PROCESS enable you to recover your CUSTOMERS' confidence and enhance their satisfaction and ENGAGEMENT?

Notes:

N1. "Customer engagement" refers to your customers' investment in your brand and product and service offerings. Characteristics of engagement include customer retention and loyalty, customers' willingness to make an effort to do business—and increase their business—with your organization, and customers' willingness to actively advocate for and recommend your brand and product and service offerings.

N2. "Product and service offerings" and "products and services" refer to the goods and services that you offer in the marketplace. Product and service offerings (3.2a) should consider all the important characteristics of products and services and their performance throughout their full life cycle and the full "consumption chain." The focus should be on features that affect customer preference and loyalty—for example, those features that differentiate your products and services from competing offerings or other organizations' services. Those features might include price, reliability, value, delivery, timeliness, ease of use, requirements for the use and disposal of hazardous materials, customer or technical support, and the sales relationship. Key product and service features also might take into account how transactions occur and factors such as the privacy and security of customer data. Your results on performance relative to key product and service features should be reported in Item 7.1, and those concerning customer perceptions and actions (outcomes) should be reported in Item 7.2.

N3. The goal of customer support (3.2a[2]) is to make your organization easy to do business with and responsive to your customers' expectations.

N4. Building customer relationships (3.2b) might include the development of partnerships or alliances with customers.

For additional description of this item, see pages 36-37.

4 Measurement, Analysis, and Knowledge Management (100 pts.)

The *Measurement, Analysis, and Knowledge Management* category examines HOW your organization selects, gathers, analyzes, manages, and improves its data, information, and KNOWLEDGE ASSETS and HOW it manages its information technology. The category also examines HOW your organization uses review findings to improve its PERFORMANCE.

4.1 Measurement, Analysis, and Improvement of Organizational Performance: How do you measure, analyze, and then improve organizational performance? (50 pts.) — Process

Describe HOW your organization measures, analyzes, reviews, and improves its PERFORMANCE through the use of data and information at all levels and in all parts of your organization.

Within your response, include answers to the following questions:

a. PERFORMANCE Measurement

(1) **Performance Measures** HOW do you select, collect, align, and integrate data and information for tracking daily operations and overall organizational PERFORMANCE, including progress relative to STRATEGIC OBJECTIVES and ACTION PLANS? What are your KEY organizational PERFORMANCE MEASURES, including KEY short-term and longer-term financial MEASURES? How frequently do you track these MEASURES? HOW do you use these data and information to support organizational decision making and INNOVATION?

(2) **Comparative Data** HOW do you select and ensure the EFFECTIVE use of KEY comparative data and information to support operational and strategic decision making and INNOVATION?

(3) **Customer Data** HOW do you select and ensure the EFFECTIVE use of VOICE-OF-THE-CUSTOMER data and information (including complaints) to support operational and strategic decision making and INNOVATION?

(4) **Measurement Agility** HOW do you ensure that your PERFORMANCE measurement system is able to respond to rapid or unexpected organizational or external changes?

b. PERFORMANCE ANALYSIS and Review

HOW do you review organizational PERFORMANCE and capabilities? HOW do you use your KEY organizational PERFORMANCE MEASURES in these reviews? What ANALYSES do you perform to support these reviews and ensure that conclusions are valid? HOW do you use these reviews to assess organizational success, competitive PERFORMANCE, financial health, and progress relative to STRATEGIC OBJECTIVES and ACTION PLANS? HOW do you use these reviews to assess your organization's ability to respond rapidly to changing organizational needs and challenges in your operating environment?

c. PERFORMANCE Improvement

(1) **Best-Practice Sharing** HOW do you use PERFORMANCE review findings to share lessons learned and best practices across organizational units and WORK PROCESSES?

(2) **Future Performance** HOW do you use PERFORMANCE review findings and KEY comparative and competitive data to project future PERFORMANCE?

(3) **Continuous Improvement and Innovation** HOW do you use organizational PERFORMANCE review findings to develop priorities for continuous improvement and opportunities for INNOVATION? HOW are these priorities and opportunities DEPLOYED to work group and functional-level operations throughout your organization? When appropriate, HOW are the priorities and opportunities DEPLOYED to your suppliers, PARTNERS, and COLLABORATORS to ensure organizational ALIGNMENT?

Notes:

N1. Performance measurement (4.1a) is used in fact-based decision making for setting and aligning organizational directions and resource use at the work unit, key process, departmental, and organizational levels.

N2. Comparative data and information (4.1a[2]) are obtained by benchmarking and by seeking competitive comparisons. "Benchmarking" refers to identifying processes and results that represent best practices and performance for similar activities, inside or outside your organization's industry. Competitive comparisons relate your organization's performance to that of competitors and other organizations providing similar products and services.

N3. Organizational performance reviews (4.1b) should be informed by organizational performance measurement and by performance measures reported throughout your Criteria Item responses, and they should be guided by the strategic objectives and action plans described in Items 2.1 and 2.2. The reviews also might be informed by internal or external Sterling assessments.

N4. Performance analysis (4.1b) includes examining performance trends; organizational, industry, and technology projections; and comparisons, cause-effect relationships, and correlations. Performance analysis should support your performance reviews, help determine root causes, and help set priorities for resource use. Accordingly, such analysis draws on all types of data: customer-related, financial and market, operational, and competitive.

N5. The results of organizational performance analysis and review should contribute to your organizational strategic planning in Category 2.

N6. Your organizational performance results should be reported in Items 7.1–7.5.

For additional description of this item, see pages 37-38.

"Using the framework of the Sterling Criteria for more than seven years, the leadership, staff and University of Florida physicians at Shands Jacksonville have worked together to position this patient-centered, caring organization to survive and excel within the rapidly changing scenarios of healthcare reform and reimbursement. This work has progressed while sustaining and enhancing our quality of care, which has earned us considerable recognition in our region."

-James R. Burkhart, President & CEO, Shands Jacksonville Medical Center
2008 Governor's Sterling Award Recipient
2011 Governor's Sterling Sustained Excellence Award

4.2 **Management of Information, Knowledge, and Information Technology:**
How do you manage your information, organizational knowledge, and information technology? (50 pts.)

Process

Describe HOW your organization builds and manages its KNOWLEDGE ASSETS. Describe HOW your organization ensures the quality and availability of needed data, information, software, and hardware for your WORKFORCE, suppliers, PARTNERS, COLLABORATORS, and CUSTOMERS.

Within your response, include answers to the following questions:

a. **Data, Information, and Knowledge Management**

(1) *Properties* HOW do you manage your organizational data, information, and knowledge to ensure the following properties?
- accuracy
- integrity and reliability
- timeliness
- security and confidentiality

(2) *Data and Information Availability* HOW do you make needed data and information available to your WORKFORCE, suppliers, PARTNERS, COLLABORATORS, and CUSTOMERS, as appropriate?

(3) *Knowledge Management* HOW do you manage organizational knowledge to accomplish the following?
- the collection and transfer of WORKFORCE knowledge
- the transfer of relevant knowledge from and to CUSTOMERS, suppliers, PARTNERS, and COLLABORATORS
- the rapid identification, sharing, and implementation of best practices
- the assembly and transfer of relevant knowledge for use in your INNOVATION and strategic planning PROCESSES

b. **Management of Information Resources and Technology**

(1) *Hardware and Software Properties* HOW do you ensure that hardware and software are reliable, secure, and user-friendly?

(2) *Emergency Availability* In the event of an emergency, HOW do you ensure the continued availability of hardware and software systems and the continued availability of data and information to EFFECTIVELY serve CUSTOMERS and business needs?

Note:

N1. Data and information access (4.2a[2]) might be via electronic or other means.

For additional description of this item, see page 38.

APPENDIX A 103

5 Workforce Focus (100 pts.)

The *Workforce Focus* category examines your ability to assess **WORKFORCE CAPABILITY** and **CAPACITY** needs and build a **WORKFORCE** environment conducive to **HIGH PERFORMANCE**. The category also examines **HOW** your organization engages, manages, and develops your **WORKFORCE** to utilize its full potential in **ALIGNMENT** with your organization's overall **MISSION**, strategy, and **ACTION PLANS**.

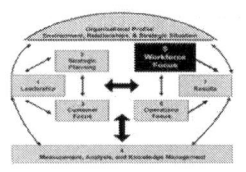

5.1 Workforce Environment: How do you build an effective and supportive workforce environment? (50 points)

Process

Describe **HOW** your organization manages **WORKFORCE CAPABILITY** and **CAPACITY** to accomplish the work of the organization. Describe **HOW** your organization maintains a safe, secure, and supportive work climate.

Within your response, include answers to the following questions:

a. **WORKFORCE CAPABILITY and CAPACITY**

(1) **Capability and Capacity** HOW do you assess your **WORKFORCE CAPABILITY** and **CAPACITY** needs, including skills, competencies, and staffing levels?

(2) **New Workforce Members** HOW do you recruit, hire, place, and retain new members of your **WORKFORCE**? HOW do you ensure that your **WORKFORCE** represents the diverse ideas, cultures, and thinking of your hiring and **CUSTOMER** community?

(3) **Work Accomplishment** HOW do you organize and manage your **WORKFORCE** to achieve the following?
- accomplish the work of your organization
- capitalize on the organization's **CORE COMPETENCIES**
- reinforce a **CUSTOMER** and business focus
- exceed **PERFORMANCE** expectations
- address your **STRATEGIC CHALLENGES** and **ACTION PLANS**

(4) **Workforce Change Management** HOW do you prepare your **WORKFORCE** for changing **CAPABILITY** and **CAPACITY** needs? HOW do you manage your **WORKFORCE**, its needs, and your needs to ensure continuity, prevent **WORKFORCE** reductions, and minimize the impact of **WORKFORCE** reductions, if they do become necessary? HOW do you prepare for and manage periods of **WORKFORCE** growth?

b. **WORKFORCE Climate**

(1) **Workplace Environment** HOW do you address workplace environmental factors, including accessibility, to ensure and improve **WORKFORCE** health, safety, and security? What are your **PERFORMANCE MEASURES** and improvement **GOALS** for each of these **WORKFORCE** needs? What are any significant differences in these factors and **PERFORMANCE MEASURES** or targets for different workplace environments?

(2) **Workforce Policies and Benefits** HOW do you support your **WORKFORCE** via policies, services, and benefits? HOW are these tailored to the needs of a diverse **WORKFORCE** and different **WORKFORCE** groups and **SEGMENTS**?

Notes:

N1. "Workforce" refers to the people actively involved in accomplishing the work of your organization. It includes your organization's permanent, temporary, and part-time personnel, as well as any contract employees supervised by your organization. It includes team leaders, supervisors, and managers at all levels. People supervised by a contractor should be addressed in Category 6 as part of your larger work systems. *For nonprofit organizations that also rely on volunteers, "workforce" includes these volunteers.*

N2. "Workforce capability" (5.1a) refers to your organization's ability to accomplish its work processes through the knowledge, skills, abilities, and competencies of its people. Capability may include the ability to build and sustain relationships with your customers; innovate and transition to new technologies; develop new products, services, and work processes; and meet changing business, market, and regulatory demands.

"Workforce capacity" (5.1a) refers to your organization's ability to ensure sufficient staffing levels to accomplish its work processes and successfully deliver your products and services to your customers, including the ability to meet seasonal or varying demand levels.

N3. Workforce capability and capacity should consider not only current needs but also future requirements based on your strategic objectives and action plans reported in Category 2.

N4. 5.1a(2) addresses only new workforce members. The retention of existing workforce members is considered in Item 5.2, Workforce Engagement.

N5. Preparing your workforce for changing capability and capacity needs (5.1a[4]) might include training, education, frequent communication, considerations of workforce employment and employability, career counseling, and outplacement and other services.

For additional description of this item, see page 39.

5.2 Workforce Engagement: How do you engage your workforce to achieve organizational and personal success? (50 pts.) — Process

Describe HOW your organization engages, compensates, and rewards your WORKFORCE to achieve HIGH PERFORMANCE. Describe HOW you assess WORKFORCE ENGAGEMENT and use the results to achieve higher PERFORMANCE. Describe HOW members of your WORKFORCE, including leaders, are developed to achieve HIGH PERFORMANCE.

Within your response, include answers to the following questions:

a. WORKFORCE PERFORMANCE

(1) **Elements of Engagement** HOW do you determine the KEY elements that affect WORKFORCE ENGAGEMENT? HOW do you determine the KEY elements that affect WORKFORCE satisfaction? HOW are these elements determined for different WORKFORCE groups and SEGMENTS?

(2) **Organizational Culture** HOW do you foster an organizational culture that is characterized by open communication, HIGH-PERFORMANCE work, and an engaged WORKFORCE? HOW do you ensure that your organizational culture benefits from the diverse ideas, cultures, and thinking of your WORKFORCE?

(3) **Performance Management** HOW does your WORKFORCE PERFORMANCE management system achieve the following?
- support HIGH-PERFORMANCE WORK and WORKFORCE ENGAGEMENT
- consider WORKFORCE compensation, reward, recognition, and incentive practices
- reinforce a CUSTOMER and business focus and achievement of your ACTION PLANS

b. Assessment of WORKFORCE ENGAGEMENT

(1) **Assessment of Engagement** HOW do you assess WORKFORCE ENGAGEMENT? What formal and informal assessment methods and MEASURES do you use to determine WORKFORCE ENGAGEMENT and WORKFORCE satisfaction? HOW do these methods and MEASURES differ across WORKFORCE groups and SEGMENTS? HOW do you use other INDICATORS, such as WORKFORCE retention, absenteeism, grievances, safety, and PRODUCTIVITY, to assess and improve WORKFORCE ENGAGEMENT?

(2) **Correlation with Business Results** HOW do you relate your WORKFORCE ENGAGEMENT assessment findings to KEY business RESULTS reported in Category 7 to identify opportunities for improvement in both WORKFORCE ENGAGEMENT and business RESULTS?

c. WORKFORCE and Leader Development

(1) **Learning and Development System** HOW does your LEARNING and development system address the following factors for your WORKFORCE members and leaders?
- your organization's CORE COMPETENCIES, STRATEGIC CHALLENGES, and accomplishment of its ACTION PLANS, both short-term and long-term
- organizational PERFORMANCE improvement and INNOVATION
- ethics and ethical business practices
- CUSTOMER focus
- their LEARNING and development needs, including those that are self-identified and those identified by supervisors, managers, and SENIOR LEADERS
- the transfer of knowledge from departing or retiring WORKFORCE members
- the reinforcement of new knowledge and skills on the job

(2) **Learning and Development Effectiveness** HOW do you evaluate the EFFECTIVENESS and efficiency of your LEARNING and development system?

(3) **Career Progression** HOW do you manage EFFECTIVE career progression for your entire WORKFORCE? HOW do you accomplish EFFECTIVE succession planning for management and leadership positions?

APPENDIX A   105

Notes:

N1. "Workforce engagement" refers to the extent of workforce commitment, both emotional and intellectual, to accomplishing the work, mission, and vision of the organization.

N2. The characteristics of "high-performance work" environments (5.2a[2] and 5.2a[3]), in which people do their utmost for the benefit of their customers and for the success of the organization, are key to understanding an engaged workforce. These characteristics are described in detail in the definition of "high-performance work" on page 51.

N3. Compensation, recognition, and related reward and incentive practices (5.2a[3]) include promotions and bonuses that might be based on performance, skills acquired, and other factors. *In some government organizations, compensation systems are set by law or regulation. However, since recognition can include monetary and non monetary, formal and informal, and individual and group mechanisms, reward and recognition systems do permit flexibility.*

N4. Identifying improvement opportunities (5.2b[2]) might draw on your workforce-focused results presented in Item 7.3 and might involve addressing workforce-related problems based on their impact on your organizational results reported in response to other Category 7 items.

N5. Your organization may have unique considerations relative to workforce development, learning, and career progression. If this is the case, your response to 5.2c should include how you address these considerations. Your response should also consider the breadth of development opportunities your organization might use, including education, training, coaching, mentoring, and work-related experiences.

For additional description of this item, see pages 39-40.

6 Operations Focus (100 pts.)

The *Operations Focus* category examines HOW your organization designs, manages, and improves its WORK SYSTEMS and WORK PROCESSES to deliver CUSTOMER VALUE and achieve organizational success and SUSTAINABILITY. Also examined is your readiness for emergencies.

6.1 Work Systems: How do you design, manage, and improve your work systems? (60 points)

Process

Describe HOW your organization designs, manages, and improves its WORK SYSTEMS to deliver CUSTOMER VALUE, prepare for potential emergencies, and achieve organizational success and SUSTAINABILITY.

Within your response, include answers to the following questions:

a. **WORK SYSTEMS DESIGN**

(1) **Design Concepts**   HOW do you design and innovate your overall WORK SYSTEMS? HOW do you capitalize on your CORE COMPETENCIES? HOW do you decide which PROCESSES within your overall WORK SYSTEMS will be internal to your organization (your KEY WORK PROCESSES) and which will use external resources?

(2) **Work System Requirements**   HOW do you determine KEY WORK SYSTEM requirements, incorporating input from CUSTOMERS, suppliers, PARTNERS, and COLLABORATORS, as appropriate? What are the KEY requirements for these WORK SYSTEMS?

b. **WORK SYSTEM Management**

(1) **Work System Implementation**   What are your organization's WORK SYSTEMS? HOW do you manage and improve your WORK SYSTEMS to deliver CUSTOMER VALUE and achieve organizational success and SUSTAINABILITY?

(2) **Cost Control**   HOW do you control the overall costs of your WORK SYSTEMS? HOW do you prevent defects, service errors, and rework and minimize warranty costs or CUSTOMERS' PRODUCTIVITY losses, as appropriate? HOW do you minimize the costs of inspections, tests, and PROCESS or PERFORMANCE audits, as appropriate?

c. **Emergency Readiness**

HOW do you ensure WORK SYSTEM and workplace preparedness for disasters or emergencies? HOW does your disaster and emergency preparedness system consider prevention, management, continuity of operations, and recovery?

Notes:

N1. "Work systems" refers to how the work of your organization is accomplished. Work systems involve your workforce, your key suppliers and partners, your contractors, your collaborators, and other components of the supply chain needed to produce and deliver your products and service and business and support processes. Your work systems coordinate the internal work processes and the external resources necessary for you to develop, produce, and deliver your products and services to your customers and to succeed in your marketplace.

N2. Disasters and emergencies (6.1c) might be weather-related, utility-related, security-related, or due to a local or national emergency, including potential pandemics. Emergency considerations related to information technology should be addressed in Item 4.2.

For additional description of this item, see page 40.

"The Florida Sterling standards will complement the existing process improvement initiatives and methodologies we use at DTCC, advancing cohesive strategic alignment across the organization while further strengthening our organizational performance and customer satisfaction."

-Eric Miller, Managing Director, The Depository Trust & Clearing Corporation (DTCC)
2011 Governor's Sterling Award Recipient

6.2 **Work Processes: How do you design, manage, and improve your work processes?** (40 points)

Process

Describe HOW your organization designs, manages, and improves its KEY WORK PROCESSES to deliver CUSTOMER VALUE and achieve organizational success and SUSTAINABILITY.

Within your response, include answers to the following questions:

a. **WORK PROCESS Design**

(1) **Design Concepts** HOW do you design and innovate your WORK PROCESSES to meet all the KEY requirements? HOW do you incorporate new technology, organizational knowledge, product and service excellence, and the potential need for agility into these PROCESSES? HOW do you incorporate CYCLE TIME, PRODUCTIVITY, cost control, and other efficiency and EFFECTIVENESS factors into these PROCESSES?

(2) **Work Process Requirements** HOW do you determine KEY WORK PROCESS requirements? What are your organization's KEY WORK PROCESSES? What are the KEY requirements for these WORK PROCESSES?

b. **WORK PROCESS Management**

(1) **Key Work Process Implementation** HOW do your KEY WORK PROCESSES relate to your WORK SYSTEMS? HOW does your day-to-day operation of these PROCESSES ensure that they meet KEY PROCESS requirements? What are your KEY PERFORMANCE MEASURES or INDICATORS and in-process MEASURES for the control and improvement of your WORK PROCESSES?

(2) **Supply-Chain Management** HOW do you manage your supply chain? HOW do you ensure that suppliers you select are qualified and positioned to enhance your PERFORMANCE and CUSTOMER satisfaction? HOW do you evaluate supplier PERFORMANCE? HOW do you deal with poorly performing suppliers?

(3) **Process Improvement** HOW do you improve your WORK PROCESSES to achieve better PERFORMANCE, reduce variability, and improve products and services?

Notes:

N1. Your key work processes (6.2a[2]) are your most important internal value creation processes and might include product and service design and delivery, customer support, supply-chain management, business, and support processes. Your key work processes are those that involve the majority of your organization's workforce members and produce customer, stakeholder, and stockholder value. "Projects" are unique work processes intended to produce an outcome and then go out of existence. Project management also may be applied to a work system challenge or opportunity.

N2. To improve process performance (6.2b[3]) and reduce variability, your organization might implement approaches such as a Lean Enterprise System, the Six Sigma methodology, ISO quality system standards, the Plan-Do-Check-Act methodology, or other process improvement tools. These approaches might be part of your performance improvement system described in response to P.2c in the Organizational Profile.

N3. The results of improvements in product and service and process performance should be reported in Item 7.1.

For additional description of this item, see page 41.

"In this economy, government organizations are expected to protect the interests of taxpayers, deliver excellence in customer service, and uphold the highest level of ethics and integrity - all while doing more work with fewer resources. Therefore, public leaders must have a razor-sharp focus on innovation and agility in our processes. This is what the Sterling Management System offers businesses, both public and private. It creates an organizational culture centered on results-oriented decisions and continually seeking better ways of doing business."

-Doug Belden, Hillsborough County Tax Collector
2008 Governor's Sterling Award Recipient
2011 Governor's Sterling Sustained Excellence Award

7 Results (360 pts.)

The RESULTS Category examines your organization's PERFORMANCE and improvement in all KEY areas—product and service and PROCESS outcomes, CUSTOMER-focused outcomes, WORKFORCE-focused outcomes, leadership and GOVERNANCE outcomes, and financial and market outcomes. PERFORMANCE LEVELS are examined relative to those of competitors and other organizations with similar product and service offerings.

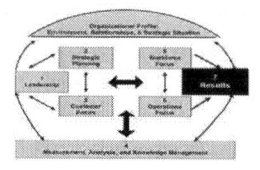

7.1 Product, Service, and Process Outcomes: What are your product and service performance and process effectiveness results? (110 pts.)

Results

Summarize your organization's KEY product and service PERFORMANCE and PROCESS EFFECTIVENESS and efficiency RESULTS. Include PROCESSES that directly serve CUSTOMERS, strategy, and operations. SEGMENT your RESULTS by product and service offerings, by CUSTOMER groups and market SEGMENTS, and by PROCESS types and locations, as appropriate. Include appropriate comparative data.

Provide data and information to answer the following questions:

a. **CUSTOMER-Focused Product and Service and PROCESS RESULTS**

What are your current LEVELS and TRENDS in KEY MEASURES or INDICATORS of product and service and PROCESS PERFORMANCE that are important to and directly serve your CUSTOMERS? How do these RESULTS compare with the PERFORMANCE of your competitors and other organizations with similar offerings?

b. **Operational PROCESS EFFECTIVENESS RESULTS**

(1) **Operational Effectiveness** What are your current LEVELS and TRENDS in KEY MEASURES or INDICATORS of the operational PERFORMANCE of your KEY WORK SYSTEMS and PROCESSES, including PRODUCTIVITY, CYCLE TIME, and other appropriate MEASURES of PROCESS EFFECTIVENESS, efficiency, and INNOVATION?

(2) **Emergency Preparedness** What are your current LEVELS and TRENDS in KEY MEASURES or INDICATORS of the EFFECTIVENESS of your WORK SYSTEM and workplace preparedness for disasters or emergencies?

c. **Strategy Implementation RESULTS**

What are your RESULTS for KEY MEASURES or INDICATORS of the accomplishment of your organizational strategy and ACTION PLANS, including building and strengthening CORE COMPETENCIES?

Notes:

N1. Results reported in Item 7.1 should provide key information for analysis and review of your organizational performance (Item 4.1); demonstrate use of organizational knowledge (Item 4.2); and provide the operational basis for customer-focused outcomes (Item 7.2) and financial and market outcomes (Item 7.5).

N2. Product and service and process results reported in 7.1a should relate to the key customer requirements and expectations identified in P.1b(2), based on information gathered in Items 3.1 and 3.2. The measures or indicators should address factors that affect customer preference, such as those included in Item P.1, Note 5, and Item 3.2, Note 2.

N3. Results reported in 7.1b should address your key operational requirements as presented in the Organizational Profile and in Items 6.1 and 6.2.

N4. Appropriate measures and indicators of operational process effectiveness (7.1b) might include audit, just-in-time delivery, and acceptance results for externally provided products, services, and processes; supplier and partner performance; product, service, and work system innovation rates and results; simplification of internal jobs and job classifications; work layout improvements; changes in supervisory ratios; response times for emergency drills or exercises; and results for work relocation or contingency exercises.

N5. Measures or indicators of strategy and action plan accomplishment (7.1c) should address your strategic objectives and goals identified in 2.1b(1) and your action plan performance measures and projected performance identified in 2.2a(5) and 2.2b, respectively.

N6. *For some nonprofit organizations, product or service performance measures might be mandated by your funding sources. These measures should be identified and reported in your response to this item.*

For additional description of this item, see page 42.

APPENDIX A

7.2 **Customer-Focused Outcomes: What are your customer-focused performance results?** (70 pts.)

Results

Summarize your organization's KEY CUSTOMER-focused RESULTS for CUSTOMER satisfaction, dissatisfaction, and ENGAGEMENT. SEGMENT your RESULTS by product and service offerings, CUSTOMER groups, and market SEGMENTS, as appropriate. Include appropriate comparative data.

Provide data and information to answer the following questions:

a. CUSTOMER-Focused RESULTS

(1) **Customer Satisfaction** What are your current LEVELS and TRENDS in KEY MEASURES or INDICATORS of CUSTOMER satisfaction and dissatisfaction? How do these RESULTS compare with the CUSTOMER satisfaction LEVELS of your competitors and other organizations providing similar products and services?

(2) **Customer Engagement** What are your current LEVELS and TRENDS in KEY MEASURES or INDICATORS of CUSTOMER ENGAGEMENT, including relationship building? How do these RESULTS compare over the course of your CUSTOMER life cycle, as appropriate?

Notes:

N1. Customer satisfaction, dissatisfaction, engagement, and relationship-building results reported in this item should relate to the customer groups and market segments discussed in P.1b(2) and Category 3 and to the listening and determination methods and data described in Item 3.1.

N2. Measures and indicators of customers' satisfaction with your products and services relative to customers' satisfaction with competitors and comparable organizations (7.2a[1]) might include information and data from your customers and from independent organizations.

For additional description of this item, see pages 42-43.

7.3 **Workforce-Focused Outcomes: What are your workforce-focused performance results?** (60 pts.)

Results

Summarize your organization's KEY WORKFORCE-focused RESULTS for your WORKFORCE environment and for WORKFORCE ENGAGEMENT. SEGMENT your RESULTS to address the DIVERSITY of your WORKFORCE and to address your WORKFORCE groups and SEGMENTS, as appropriate. Include appropriate comparative data.

Provide data and information to answer the following questions:

a. WORKFORCE RESULTS

(1) **Workforce Capability and Capacity** What are your current LEVELS and TRENDS in KEY MEASURES of WORKFORCE CAPABILITY and CAPACITY, including staffing levels and appropriate skills?

(2) **Workforce Climate** What are your current LEVELS and TRENDS in KEY MEASURES or INDICATORS of your WORKFORCE CLIMATE, including WORKFORCE health, safety, and security and WORKFORCE services and benefits, as appropriate?

(3) **Workforce Engagement** What are your current LEVELS and TRENDS in KEY MEASURES or INDICATORS of WORKFORCE ENGAGEMENT and WORKFORCE satisfaction?

(4) **Workforce Development** What are your current LEVELS and TRENDS in KEY MEASURES or INDICATORS of WORKFORCE climate and leader development?

Notes:

N1. Results reported in this item should relate to processes described in Category 5. Your results should be responsive to key work process needs described in Category 6 and to your organization's action plans and human resource or workforce plans described in Item 2.2.

N2. Responses to 7.3a(3) should include measures and indicators identified in response to 5.2b(1).

N3. *Nonprofit organizations that rely on volunteers should include results for their volunteer workforce, as appropriate.*

For additional description of this item, see page 43.

7.4 Leadership and Governance Outcomes: What are your senior leadership and governance results? (60 pts.)

Results

Summarize your organization's KEY SENIOR LEADERSHIP and GOVERNANCE RESULTS, including those for fiscal accountability, legal compliance, ETHICAL BEHAVIOR, societal responsibility, and support of KEY communities. SEGMENT your RESULTS by organizational units, as appropriate. Include appropriate comparative data.

Provide data and information to answer the following questions:

a. Leadership, GOVERNANCE, and Societal Responsibility RESULTS

(1) **Leadership** What are your RESULTS for KEY MEASURES or INDICATORS of SENIOR LEADERS' communication and engagement with the WORKFORCE to DEPLOY VISION and VALUES, encourage two-way communication, and create a focus on action?

(2) **Governance** What are your KEY current findings and TRENDS in KEY MEASURES or INDICATORS of GOVERNANCE and fiscal accountability, internal and external, as appropriate?

(3) **Law and Regulation** What are your RESULTS for KEY MEASURES or INDICATORS of achieving and surpassing regulatory and legal requirements?

(4) **Ethics** What are your RESULTS for KEY MEASURES or INDICATORS of ETHICAL BEHAVIOR and of STAKEHOLDER trust in your organization's SENIOR LEADERS and GOVERNANCE? What are your RESULTS for KEY MEASURES or INDICATORS of breaches of ETHICAL BEHAVIOR?

(5) **Society** What are your RESULTS for KEY MEASURES or INDICATORS of your organization's fulfillment of its societal responsibilities and your organization's support of its KEY communities?

Items 6.1 and 6.2. Include results not reported in Items 7.1–7.4.

Notes:

N1. Responses to 7.4a(1) should address communication processes identified in Item 1.1.

N2. Responses to 7.4a(2) might include financial statement issues and risks, important internal and external auditor recommendations, and the management's responses to these matters. *For some nonprofit organizations, results of IRS 990 audits also might be included.*

N3. Regulatory and legal results (7.4a[3]) should address requirements described in 1.2b. Workforce-related occupational health and safety results (e.g., Occupational Safety and Health Administration [OSHA] reportable incidents) should be reported in 7.3a(2).

N4. For examples of measures of ethical behavior and stakeholder trust (7.4a[4]), see Item 1.2, note 4.

N5. Responses to 7.4a(5) should address your organization's societal responsibilities described in 1.2b(1) and 1.2c(1), as well as support of the key communities described in 1.2c(2). Measures of contributions to societal well-being might include reduced energy consumption; the use of renewable energy resources, recycled water, and alternative approaches to conserving resources (e.g., increased audio and video conferencing); and the global use of enlightened labor practices.

For additional description of this item, see page 43.

APPENDIX A 111

7.5 **Financial and Market Outcomes: What are your financial and marketplace performance results? (60 pts.)**

Results

Summarize your organization's KEY financial and marketplace PERFORMANCE RESULTS by market SEGMENTS or CUSTOMER groups, as appropriate. Include appropriate comparative data.

Provide data and information to answer the following questions:

a. **Financial and Market RESULTS**

  (1) **Financial Performance** What are your current LEVELS and TRENDS in KEY MEASURES or INDICATORS of financial PERFORMANCE, including aggregate MEASURES of financial return, financial viability, or budgetary PERFORMANCE, as appropriate?

  (2) **Marketplace Performance** What are your current LEVELS and TRENDS in KEY MEASURES or INDICATORS of marketplace PERFORMANCE, including market share or position, market and market share growth, and new markets entered, as appropriate?

Notes:

N1. Responses to 7.5a(1) should include aggregate measures of financial return, such as return on investment (ROI), operating margins, profitability, or profitability by market segment or customer group. Responses also should include measures of financial viability, such as liquidity, debt-to-equity ratio, days cash on hand, asset utilization, and cash flow. Measures should relate to the financial measures reported in 4.1a(1) and the financial management approaches described in Item 2.2. For nonprofit organizations, additional measures might include performance to budget, reserve funds, cost avoidance or savings, administrative expenditures as a percentage of budget, and the cost of fundraising versus funds raised.

N2. For nonprofit organizations, responses to 7.5a(2) might include measures of charitable donations or grants and the number of new programs or services offered.

For additional description of this item, see page 43.

112 SERVANT GOVERNING

APPENDIX B

MARION COUNTY SHERIFF'S OFFICE SUSTAINED EXCELLENCE AWARD APPLICATION (2011)

A PUBLIC DOCUMENT

MARION COUNTY SHERIFF'S OFFICE

THE JOURNEY CONTINUES

GOVERNOR'S STERLING SUSTAINED PERFORMANCE EXELLENCE AWARD

Table of Contents

Sterling Sustained Performance Excellence Award Application Form............I

Organizational Chart..II

Organizational Profile..III

Organizational Profile Addendum...VIII

Criteria Changes...1

Opportunities for Improvement..9

7.0   **Organizational Performance Results**
    7.1 Product and Service Outcomes..16
    7.2 Customer-Focused Outcomes..18
    7.3 Financial and Market Outcomes...19
    7.4 Workforce Focused Outcomes..21
    7.5 Process Effectiveness Outcomes..24
    7.6 Leadership and Outcomes...27

Glossary of Terms and
Abbreviations...XIII

Sterling Sustained Performance Excellence Award Application

2011 Governor's Sterling Sustained Performance Excellence Award Application Form

GENERAL INSTRUCTIONS

Please update any information that has changed since the Application of Intent and type or very clearly print all information requested. It is recommended that the application be submitted to the Sterling office electronically.

ITEM INSTRUCTIONS

Item 1 – Applicant — Provide the official name and mailing address of the organization applying for the Award.

1. Applicant Official Name

Organization Name: Marion County Sheriff's Office

Address: P.O. Box 1987, Ocala, FL 34478

Item 2 – Official Inquiry Point — As the examination proceeds, the Administrator may need to contact the Applicant for additional information. Give the name, address, and telephone number of the official with authority to provide additional information or to arrange a Site Visit. If this official contact point changes during the course of the Application process, please inform the Florida Sterling Council.

2. Official Inquiry Point

Name: Kerry Crawford

Title: Major

Mailing Address: P.O. Box 1987, Ocala, FL 34478

Overnight Mailing Address: 692 NW 30th Ave, Ocala, FL 34475

Telephone Number: 352-369-6831

Fax Number: 352-438-5973   Email Address: kcrawford@marionso.com

Item 3 – Fees —
Application of Intent Fee $100 (Submit with Application of Intent)
Application Fee $2,500 (Submit with application)
Site Visit Examiners' Expenses TBD (Billed after site visit)

3. Fee (see instructions)

Make check or money order payable to the **Florida Sterling Council** for $2,500 and mail it to the Sterling office.

Item 4 – Release Statement — Please read this section carefully. A signed Application indicates that the Applicant agrees to the terms and conditions stated therein.

4. Release Statement

We understand this application will be reviewed by members of the Board of Examiners. We agree to participate in conference calls and to host the Site Visit and facilitate an open and unbiased examination. We understand that Site Visit expenses will be determined in accordance with the section: *Fees*, Page 7, *2011 Governor's Sterling Sustained Performance Excellence Award Guidelines and Application Forms*

Item 5 – Authorizing Official — The signature of the Applicant's highest ranking management official or designee is required and indicates the Applicant will comply with the terms and conditions stated in the document.

5. Signature, Authorizing Official: *[signature]*

Name: Ed Dean

Title: Sheriff

Address: P.O. Box 1987, Ocala, FL 34478

Date: January 13, 2011   Telephone Number: 352-368-6831

Organizational Chart

APPENDIX B 119

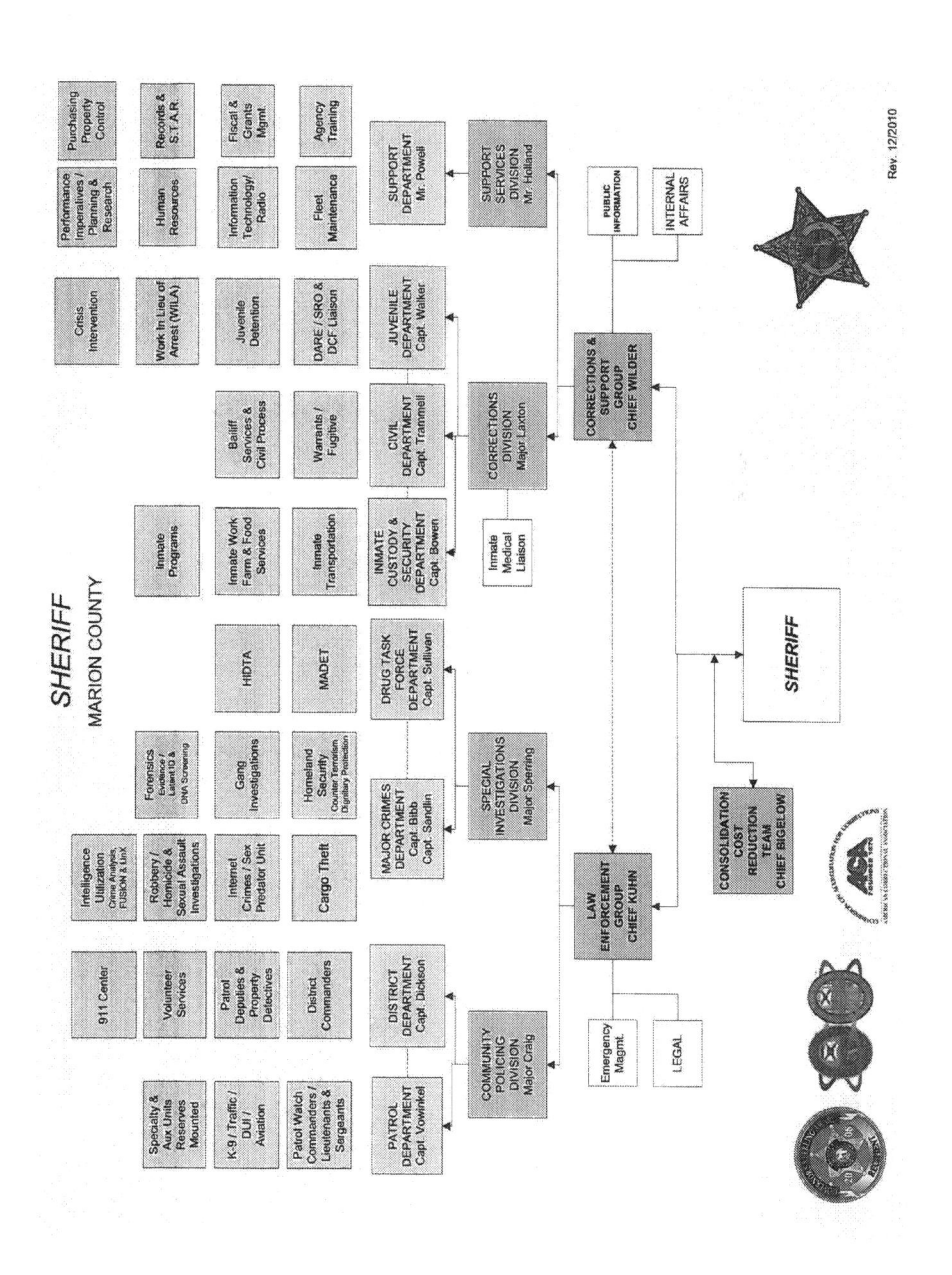

Organizational Profile

Organizational Profile

The Florida State Constitution and Chapter 30, Florida Statutes, outlines the powers, duties and responsibilities of the Sheriff's Office, which are promulgated through the election of a Sheriff in each respective jurisdiction or county. Sheriffs' offices throughout the state will vary in structure and services provided.

P.1a.(1). Main Product and Services
The main products and services of the Marion County Sheriff's Office (MCSO) are law enforcement and corrections. These are also considered our core competencies.

Law Enforcement: The delivery of law enforcement services to our customers is accomplished through the Law Enforcement Group.

Corrections: The delivery of corrections services is accomplished through the Corrections Group, which also encompasses the Court Services function.

attendance of all terms of circuit and county courts. Our vision is to be a "premier, value centered Sheriff's Office that is recognized for excellence in service by Putting Citizens First". Our vision is accomplished through four Guiding Strategies. These Guiding Strategies (Table P.1.2.) enable us to focus on creating and balancing value for the customers and key stakeholders. The progress toward achieving our vision is accomplished by evaluating the key performance measures which are aligned to each Guiding Strategy. We define "premier" as performance on these eleven measures that are comparable to or exceeding the "Best Florida Peers" and organizations who have been identified as role models through the Florida Governor's Sterling Award (Table P.1.2).

P.1.a (3). Workforce Profile:
MCSO's workforce includes 828 current employees, segmented by sworn officers (529, 65%) and civilians (299, 35%). Key requirements and expectations include employee satisfaction with their job (Figure 7.4.2), the development of skills for improvement and advancement (Figure 7.4.3), and for the employees to have the necessary tools and

SERVANT LEADERSHIP					
MCSO inverts the organizational pyramid through the concept of Servant Leadership. The Sheriff serves the employees of the Sheriff's Office, and together, the Sheriff and the Sheriff's Office employees serve the people of Marion County. Servant Leadership principles are:					
Listening	Healing	Persuasion	Foresight	Building community	
Empathy	Awareness	Conceptualization	Stewardship	Commitment to the growth of people	
MISSION STATEMENT					
"We pledge to serve with honor and to diligently protect the quality of life in Marion County through community policing".					
VISION STATEMENT					
"The vision of the MCSO is to be a premier, value centered Sheriff's Office that is recognized for excellence in service by putting citizens first."					
CORE VALUES					
Neatness	Pride	Achievement	Punctuality	Respect	Responsibility
Brotherhood	Shame	Discipline	Persistence	Loyalty	Courage

Table P. 1.1

The groups identified within the two core competencies are considered our key work processes. Key process requirements and performance measures are identified in **Tables 6.1.1 and 6.1.3.**

P.1,a(2). Organizational Culture, Purpose, Vision, Mission, and Values
MCSO's culture is a value-centered agency which subscribes to a servant leadership approach in dealing with its personnel and the public it serves.

The purpose of the Sheriff's Office includes the apprehension of any person disturbing the peace or committing a crime and presenting that person before a proper judicial officer; execution of writs, processes, warrants and other papers, for housing pre-sentenced and sentenced criminal offenders and

qualifications to perform their duties (Figure 7.4.4).

As shown in Table P.1.3, diversity of the workforce is reflective of the community it serves (Figure 7.4.5). The workforce possesses a variety of educational backgrounds including PhDs, JDs, Masters, Bachelors, Associate, and College/High School/Vo-Tech (Table P.1.4).

The patrol deputies of the Marion County Sheriff's Office have recently voted in the Fraternal Order of Police as a collective bargaining unit. Contract negotiation is pending at the time of this writing.

MCSO offers a variety of benefits, which includes, but is not limited to pension, sick leave, vacation leave, retirement, personal day, educational achievement pay, tuition reimbursement, flexible spending account, deductible

Organizational Profile

GUIDING STRATEGIES	Description	Key Performance Measures
QUALITY OF LIFE	MCSO will strive to improve the quality of life of the citizens of Marion County by maintaining a low crime rate and a high crime clearance rate, thus fostering a sense of peace and security in the community.	• Figure 7.1.1 Part 1 Crime rate per 1,000 • Figure 7.1.2 Crime clearance rate • Figure 7.1.3 Escapes from Correction facility
STEWARDSHIP	MCSO is committed to maximizing the use of public tax dollars in the delivery of quality-driven, appropriate, and cost effective law enforcement services to the citizens by ensuring fiscal responsibility for financial resources received from the county, state, and federal government.	• Figure 7.3.1 Law enforcement cost per capita • Figure 7.3.2 Average inmate cost per day
SAFE AND MOTIVATED WORK FORCE	MCSO promotes a work environment where officer and employee safety, personal development, specialized training, and the use of state of the art technology are deployed in order to achieve the agency's mission and vision.	• Figure 7.4.8 Average Worker's Compensation Incidents per employee • Figure 7.4.1 Employee Satisfaction • Figure 7.4.6 Employee Retention
EXCELLENCE OF SERVICE	MCSO will continue to raise the standard of excellence in the service it provides to the citizens	• Figure 7.1.6 Overall Citizen Satisfaction • Figure 7.2.1 Overall satisfied with response by SO • Figure 7.2.2 Overall satisfied with the way call handled

Table P.1.2

insurance packages, and a step pay plan for sworn corrections and law enforcement officers.

Demographic	Marion County	MCSO
White	75.8%	79%
Black	12.1%	13.6%
Hispanic	9.6%	6%
Asian	1.4%	.02%
Other	1.1%	.02%
Total Males	48.6%	49.7%
Total Females	51.4%	51.3%
Total Population	328,547	828

Table P.1.3 (MCSO demographics)

Key health and safety requirements include Workers' Compensation Florida Statute 440, and various Law Enforcement and Correction standards listed in Table P.1.5.

MCSO utilizes volunteers who work throughout the agency in various capacities based on volunteer expertise and organizational needs. These contributions include clerical functions, crime watch groups, funeral escort, homeland security, bailiffs and others.

P.1.a. (4). Facilities, Technology and Equipment

Facilities: The Marion County Sheriff's Office Criminal Justice Complex is comprised of several buildings which include the Sheriff's Main Operations Center, Marion County Fleet and Radio Maintenance, Emergency Operations Center, Communications Center, and the Central Warehouse.

Education

[Pie chart: High School 50.54%, Some College 22.97%, Associates 11.25%, Bachelors 9.55%, Masters 3.75%, Doctorate 0.36%, GED 1.57%]

Table P.1.4

MCSO Law Enforcement operations are decentralized in support of community oriented policing. The philosophy is supported through 12 districts, which operate from 9 offices strategically located throughout the county. Some personnel are assigned to other county facilities such as the courthouse (Court Services) and the airport (Aviation and Drug Unit).

Equipment and Technology: In addition to patrol vehicles, radios and firearms; MCSO issues tasers, in-car cameras/video equipment, cell phones, mobile data terminals (MDTs), ballistic shields, riot gear, radar units, stop sticks, hazardous response gear, bulletproof vests, Rapid ID system (fingerprint scanners), GPS, LinX, PDAs (for documenting security

Organizational Profile

checks), and archive fingerprint system (allows prints to be transferred electronically).

The Mobile Command Center, is a deployable emergency communications hub, which is equipped with multiple communications mediums, mapping and video downlink capabilities, providing full communications capabilities on site at any crime scene or disaster site. There are two OH58 helicopters, both of which are equipped with thermal imaging capabilities, 10 million candle-power spotlights, video downlink, and an aero-moving map system. Many of our specialty units utilize task-specific equipment including vans, robots, boats, as well as other equipment and technology. There are 709 agency vehicles which are maintained by an in-house maintenance facility.

P.1.a (5). Regulatory Environment:

MCSO operates under both federal and state regulatory requirements. All sworn law enforcement and corrections staff must meet State certification and training requirements (Figure 7.6.7) as outlined by the Florida Criminal Justice Standards and Training Commission (CJSTC). Due to taking over the housing of the juvenile inmates in Marion County in 2010, we undergo quarterly Department of Juvenile Justice inspections. Industry accreditation is not a required regulatory process; however, MCSO is accredited in both law enforcement and corrections and complies with these accreditation standards. Law Enforcement accreditation has been obtained from the Commission for Florida Law Enforcement Accreditation (CFA). The Bomb Squad and K9 Unit are separately accredited. Accreditation for corrections has been obtained from both the Florida Corrections Accreditation Commission (FCAC) and the Commission on Accreditation for Corrections (ACA). MCSO has currently undergone the Commission on Accreditation for Law Enforcement Agencies, Inc. (CALEA) process for initial national accreditation for Law Enforcement and Communications (Figure 7.6.8).

P.1.b.(1). Organizational Relationships:

The Sheriff is the Chief Law Enforcement Officer of the county and is the Chief Executive Officer of MCSO. As an elected official and a constitutional officer, a Sheriff answers to the citizens within the jurisdiction he/she serves. The Sheriff obtains the budget to operate from the Marion County Board of County Commission. There are Chiefs of Staff who report directly to the Sheriff and oversee the operation of the two groups, which are then split into divisions (P.1.a (1).

P.1.b (2). Customers and Requirements:

The Guiding Strategy of Excellence of Service is how we focus our efforts towards "Putting Citizens First". MCSO identifies the citizens of Marion County as the key customer group and provides law enforcement and correction services on their behalf. Through the numerous listening posts described in the original GSA application and customer focus groups, MCSO has identified the key customer requirements and measures listed in Table P.1.6.

P.1.b (3). Suppliers, Partners

MCSO identifies key suppliers and partners as organizations who contribute significantly towards achievement of the Guiding Strategies and measures used to monitor performance with each. The supply chain requirements are listed below for the key suppliers.

Key Supplier:
- **Executive Information Services (EIS):** Develops key organizational software and updates.
- **Ocala Community Care:** A not-for-profit organization providing inmate healthcare service at a reduced cost to taxpayers(Table 6.1.3, 7.3.9);

Key Partners:
- **Multi-Agency Drug Enforcement Team (MADET) /High-Intensity Drug Trafficking Area (HIDTA):** A partnership of local, state and federal law enforcement agencies working together to combat illegal drug and vice activity (Table 6.1.3, Figure 7.5.5);
- **FDLE:** Assisted in the implementation of the DNA screening lab which has reduced the Forensic evidence examination turn-around time. (Table 6.1.3, Figure 7.5.2).

P.1.b (4). Communication:

Key customer partnering and communication mechanisms are

Regulatory	Agency	Measures
Federal	• EEOC • ADA • Fair Labor Standards Act • Federal Communications Commission • Uniform Crime Reporting (UCR)	• Figure 7.6.6 Number of Substantiated EEOC Complaints • Figure 7.6.7 Meet Certification and Training Requirements
State	• Florida State Statutes • Florida Department of Law Enforcement Standards • Commission for Florida Law Enforcement Accreditation • Commission on Accreditation for Corrections • Florida Corrections Accreditation Commission • Florida Model Jail Standards	• Figure 7.6.8 Law Enforcement Accreditation compliance • Figure 7.6.8 Corrections Accreditation compliance

Table P.1.5 Regulatory Agencies

APPENDIX B

Organizational Profile

described in the original GSA application. Supplier and partnering communication occurs through designated liaisons for each group through a variety of mediums, such as phone, email, face-to-face contact and committee participation.

Law enforcement and corrections comparisons are made with sheriff's offices identified as our "Best Florida Peers". There are limited industry standards determining law enforcement and correction measurements. Some comparable data is different in the way it is collected, measured and analyzed

Key Customer	Key Requirements and Measures
Citizens of Marion County	• Response time: Figure 7.2.4 They responded in a reasonable time • Visibility: Figure 7.2.1. Overall satisfied with response • Problem solving and Communications: Figure 7.2.2 Overall you were satisfied the way call was handled • Professional service: Figure 7.2.3 The employee was professional and helpful

Table P.1.6

	Strategic challenges	Strategic advantages
Operational	Down-turned economy has led to budgetary constraints which challenge us to continue to maintain our high level of service provided to our customers.	Flexibility, partnerships, listening posts, technology, accountability, Quality Review Teams, performance, decentralization.
Human resource	Down-turned economy has led to budget constraints which affect our ability to maintain proper compensation of our employees.	Innovative strategies; for example increased paid leave allowances and implemented a new step pay plan for sworn officers.
Organizational sustainability	Down-turned economy has led to budget constraints which could lead to the above operational and human resource challenges. These two areas have a direct impact on our key performance measures.	Customer satisfaction, agility, innovation, vision, strategic planning, transparency, accessibility, commitment to maintaining current staff.

Table P.1.7

P.2.a.(1). Competitive Environment
Due to the constitutional structure and geographical boundaries of sheriff's offices in the State of Florida, MCSO does not have a competitor for law enforcement or corrections services. The growth and decrease for law enforcement and corrections services since 2007 are:

- 18% decrease in jail inmate population
- 1.3% increase in citizen population
- 11% increase in calls for law enforcement services

P.2.a.(2). Principal Factors
Although we don't have competitors, the principal factor that determines our success with citizens is our ability to demonstrate achievement of our four Guiding Strategies, and the key measures and targets aligned to each (Table P.1.2). The key challenge that impacts our ability to achieve our Guiding Strategies is the down-turned economy. This challenge has forced opportunities for innovation to be even more cost effective. (see examples of innovation in P.2.1).

P.2.a (3). Comparative Data
The key sources for comparative data within the law enforcement core competency include the Florida Department of Law Enforcement (FDLE), and the Federal Bureau of Investigation (FBI). Key sources of comparative data outside the industry include Florida Governor's Sterling Award winning organizations, which are recognized as being role models.

among agencies. Limitations in obtaining data include whether or not other agencies track the data and their willingness to share data collection methodology. Some of MCSO's performance measures are agency specific and are not tracked by other criminal justice organizations in Florida.

MCSO's primary use of comparative data is to identify "Best Florida Peer" or "Role Model" status for each of the key measures aligned to the four Guiding Strategies (Table P.1.2) and is used to assess our progress towards MCSO's vision to maintain "premier" status.

P.2 b. Strategic Challenges
Restricted funding affects our ability to respond to population growth and associated staffing requirements. As an example, in response to reduced funding, a community based group of health care providers (Ocala Community Care partnership) was assembled and has kept our average cost of inmate per day among the lowest in the state of Florida (Figure 7.3.2). MCSO has partnered with the Department of Juvenile Justice (DJJ) to transition the housing of incarcerated juveniles in Marion County from the custody of DJJ to MCSO. This initiative brought about a $3.2 million dollar annual savings to the taxpayer. Strategic advantages are identified annually during the SWOT analysis, as part of the strategic planning process (Table P.1.7)

P.2 c. Performance Improvement System
Each division has key performance improvement processes, which includes:

Organizational Profile

Monthly Updates and Quarterly "STAT Meetings": MCSO's organizational philosophy incorporates a monthly review of statistical data (business results) pertinent to the key processes which contribute to the mission, which is also examined quarterly by senior staff. These reviews allow the agency to evaluate trends, problems, and solutions with a focus on performance improvement. Along with employee feedback, this quarterly review is a systematic evaluation of key processes by providing a look at key performance indicators. Other daily, weekly, and monthly reviews help expand these evaluations.

Quality Review Teams: Quality Review Teams meet monthly and contribute to performance improvement efforts within that group. All Quality Review Teams utilize a continuous process improvement model, and incorporate process mapping to ensure consistency and continuity of performance. These innovations are discussed in presentations with the Command Staff. Employee engagement is enhanced by rotating line level people within those teams to capture diverse ideas. Also, representatives from the seven QRT's meet quarterly to transfer knowledge and learning, to obtain cross-functional input and conduct peer review with other Quality Review Teams.

Strategic Action Plan Review and Revision: When appropriate, the Strategic Action Plan may be modified or adjusted to meet current needs within the agency and the community. This promotes agency agility and continuous cycles of improvement.

Rapid Process Improvements: MCSO has adopted the Six Sigma RPI process improvement tool. We have applied this tool to reduce rework and duplication.

Adoption Florida Sterling Model: MCSO has a proven ability to manage and integrate a large number of complex accreditation systems within the best management framework of Sterling. MCSO has a proven record of efficiency and is a performance-based organization utilizing Sterling Management principles. MCSO has had numerous national and state assessors conduct on-site accreditation assessments of our practices to ensure we are operating at the highest industry standards. MCSO is a multi-accredited and recognized first responder organization with a true commitment by all of the employees for "Putting Citizens First."

Growth Support: MCSO encourages personal learning by providing an educational reimbursement program, educational incentive pay, and a computer lab for employee use. Training is also provided relevant to the needs of the employee and the agency.

MCSO has a history of continuous improvement for the customers, as demonstrated in Table P.2.1.

Years	Key Tasks/Activities
'06-'07	- K-9, Aviation & Traffic (KAT) Stats Implemented - Major Crimes Stats (M-Stat) Implemented - Corrections/Inmate Booking Survey - Female Inmate Work Farm - DNA Screening Lab - Energy Committee - Inmate/Community Healthcare - Collaboration DNA Screening Lab - Inmate/Community Healthcare Collaboration
'07-'08	- Refined inmate care process by switching to OCC - Suicide prevention innovation - Video Visitation - Sergeant Customer Satisfaction Surveys - District Customer Satisfaction Surveys
'08-'09	- Refined IT process by switching to internal IT and EIS - Six Sigma Process Management - New Emergency Operations Center - High Intensity Patrol areas created - American Correctional Association
'09-'10	- Consolidation proposal for Fire Services - Streamline organization - Take-over of DJJ and JAC duties - Solar farm (energy savings) - CALEA accreditation for Law Enforcement & Communications - Sworn employees step pay plan - 911 emergency texting - New Communication Center - Silent Dispatch concept Implemented

Table P.2.1. Continuous Improvement

Organizational Profile Addendum

Organizational Profile Addendum

Organizational Sustainability

What can you point to that will lead us to think this organization will be operating and in good health in 10 years from now? 20 years from now?

As described in the profile, MCSO's strategic advantages include customer satisfaction, agility, innovation, vision, strategic planning, transparency, accessibility, and a commitment to maintaining current staff.

Significant examples of innovative and visionary thinking include:
- Adoption of the Sterling Management principles. MCSO was the first Law Enforcement/Corrections agency to utilize the model which has led to MCSO being considered as a role model to other agencies.
- The development and implementation of the inmate healthcare model, Ocala Community Care (OCC) as described in P.2.b
- The organization's statistical approach and review process provides accountability and helps MCSO remain current and maintain high levels of performance in response to customer needs. This process is ingrained for future leaders.
- The proposal to consolidate Marion County Fire Rescue Services under the auspices of MCSO is a cost savings idea for the taxpayer as well as a means to improve functionality and efficiency for public safety. This model is still under consideration by the County Commission. (OFI 2.1.a.1)

In addition, the following contributes to MCSO's long-term sustainability:
- A short term and long term application of a strategic planning process to include an evaluation of Strengths, Weaknesses, Opportunities, and Threats (SWOT) throughout the organization.
- The organization's Quality Review Team's (QRT's) promote process improvements and also provide a foundation for future leader development.
- Rapid Process Improvement (RPI's) tools provide for line-level employee input into streamlining workplace strategies.

MCSO's Multiyear Plan is developed to guide the annual strategic plan for long term goals. It is intended to be a flexible document. Events and budgetary constraints can significantly alter prospective resources and timelines.

Improved Governance

Name three major recent improvements to your governance that has lessened systematic risk, increased your ability to handle disruptions and position the organization for future growth and/or sustainability.

- As seen in the organizational chart, from the previous GSA application to the current one, MCSO has streamlined the organization from eight Bureaus to four Divisions. In lieu of terminating employees as other agencies have done, a commitment was made to maintain current staff members. The organization has instead reduced staff levels through attrition, freezing vacancies, and restricting promotions. Adopting a "do more with less" philosophy and a reallocation of some work systems and resources have contributed as well. Across the United States citizens have asked for "less taxes"; but do not want a reduction in services. MCSO has accomplished this for the customers by implementing these practices without a reduction in performance levels.

- In 2010 the Marion County Commission requested a $3.2 million dollar budget cut from MCSO Corrections. This would have been devastating to the operation of the Corrections core competency. In seeking alternatives to ensure sustainability, MCSO discovered that the Marion County Board of County Commissioners was budgeting for the State of Florida Department of Juvenile Justice $3.2 million per year to house pre-trial juvenile offenders. MCSO chose to assume this responsibility from the Department of Juvenile Justice without increasing MCSO's budget. After a lengthy approval process, which included developing acceptable processes, training, and a minimal reallocation of personnel, the venture was approved by the State of Florida. The savings to the Marion County Board of County Commissioners, who in the past were required to budget this amount yearly, was credited to the MCSO's budget for the 2010/2011 fiscal year replacing the request to reduce the Organization's budget. Due to the success of the collaboration with DJJ, other agencies are now looking at MCSO's new, innovative model as a means of potential budget savings.

MCSO also assumed the responsibilities of the Juvenile Assessment Center (JAC) for processing juvenile arrestees in Marion County. This includes medical screening, psychological evaluation, fingerprinting, and coordinating detention screening. This resulted in a savings of $280,000 to the taxpayers of Marion County.

- MCSO discovered a rise in inmate suicides. In response, a nationally recognized expert was contracted to evaluate MCSO's practices and make recommendations for improvement. These recommendations included:
    a. Additional staff training to include; recognition, indicators, and coping strategies.
    b. Equipment modifications such as wall mount bunks, clothing, identification methods, and increased inmate monitoring.
    c. Policy and protocol changes.

Organizational Profile Addendum

There has not been an inmate suicide since these changes were implemented. In addition, the United States Department of Justice conducted a review of MCSO's operation and found no constitutional violations. To ensure continuous learning, the expert returns for follow-up training and evaluation on a regular basis to ensure MCSO is applying best practices.

Culture Change with regard to continuous learning/experimenting

What are the signs that the Agency has embraced a culture of continuous learning?

- A review of MCSO's Customer Satisfaction Survey process, along with the GSA Feedback Report, revealed a lack of segmentation. Moreover, it was deemed MCSO could develop a process which would reflect a more timely rating. Patrol sergeants are now required to randomly poll a minimum number of customers per month who are segmented by grid and district to obtain immediate feedback on job performance. These contacts are made soon after the deputy completes a call for service. Additionally, each District Office now has citizen survey cards available for the customers to complete. This provides segmented data for the District Commanders' timely assessment of the performance of their officers. A hard copy of the compiled data is distributed monthly. Recently a process enhancement has been initiated to develop an electronic process for more immediate access for both survey completion and review. (Figure 7.1.6)

- The organization utilizes Quality Review Teams (QRTs) at the Division level consisting of line level employees, who look for ways to improve the organizations performance, correct or improve a process deficiency, and make changes to the process if necessary. Quality Review Teams exist in eight strategically selected venues within the MCSO and function as outlined in P2.c. The RPI tool is open to all divisions within the MCSO, and is strongly an actionable mechanism employed by the line-level employees. Moreover, the QRT philosophy and RPI sessions most closely resemble learning models that the Senior Staff eagerly support.

- The Corrections Group has initiated a customer survey relating to the release of inmates (Table PA 1.2). The initial survey results led to an improvement of services which has recently been reflected in more favorable ratings. The Corrections QRT reviewed the survey results and recommended the use of the Rapid Process Improvement method to evaluate the booking release process stream. This session led to a streamlined inmate release process. This survey is repeated yearly and has shown improvement in the process areas of video visitation and booking release.

- Statistical evaluations are important to the MCSO. On certain occasions, statistical evaluation calls for additional strategies. The High Intensity Patrol (HIP) is a clear example of statistical reviews that led to actionable strategies. A review of the stats at the Northwest District Office revealed a rising trend of burglaries. HIP zones were created and as a result, burglaries in that area were reduced by 37% (CC Table 3.1).

Describe some of the Agency innovations or experiments that you have tried and what are the results of those innovations and experiments?

- Due to changing technology, MCSO developed a 911 texting protocol (May 2010) where-in an individual can text the Marion County Sheriff's Office Communications Center if they need help in an emergency. MCSO is the first organization in the United States to offer this service which has saved the life of one individual already.

- The "Inmate welfare line" was developed as a process to enable inmate's families (customers) to have direct, timely access to the Corrections Division's Watch Commander. The process includes both a direct phone line and email connection accessible through the MCSO web-site. This new process has reduced inmate grievance complaints, because supervisors are dispatched one-on-one to speak to inmates and resolve concerns prior to reaching grievance levels (Table PA 1.1)

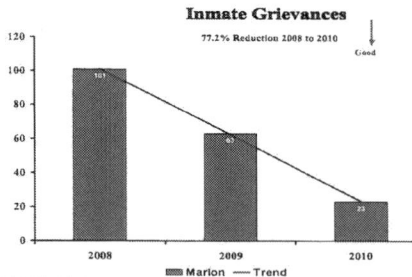

Inmate Grievances
77.2% Reduction 2008 to 2010 — Good

(Bar chart: 2008 = 101, 2009 = 49, 2010 = 23; Marion — Trend)

Table PA 1.1

- The jail video visitation facility has streamlined the process for visiting an inmate at the Marion County Jail. The addition of the video system allows family members to schedule visits with inmates. This facility is open to the public and is detached from the Marion County Corrections jail. This eliminates the need to bring family members into the secure facility. Prior to this implementation the process created long waits and customer dissatisfaction. The new approach has minimized wait times and reduced the introduction of contraband.

- GPS systems in the patrol car mobile data terminal (MDT) enables the communication center, patrol deputies and patrol supervisors to monitor each unit's location and assist in managing the proper selection of patrol units to dispatch to calls. An additional GPS system in patrol vehicles enable the

Organizational Profile Addendum

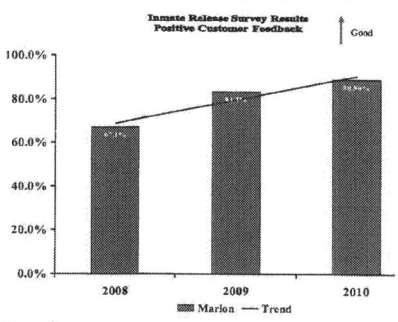

Inmate Release Survey Results Positive Customer Feedback ↑ Good

[Bar chart showing 2008, 2009, 2010 with upward trend]

Table PA 1.2

patrol deputies to determine the quickest route to respond to calls for service. This has assisted in the reduction of response time, a key customer requirement. (Figure 7.1.5)

- A kiosk was added in the video visitation room to allow inmate's families and friends to deposit monies into an inmate's welfare account. The system assists the customer, provides accountability, and lessened manpower needs to manage the inmate account.

- An in-house energy conversation committee explored the possibility of adding solar panels to the corrections facility to reduce energy costs. Federal stimulus money became available to install a solar water heater system. Timers were also placed on the inmate showers and toilets. This project is not completed, but projected cost savings are estimated at $150,000 annually.

- During the economic downturn and reduction of operating capital, the organization was able to come up with several innovations to compensate the organizations employees when pay raises were not given.

- Each employee was given an additional 40 hours of paid leave to be taken during the fiscal year 2009/2010.

- Each employees was given the opportunity to earn and be paid up to $500 dollars of unused annual /compensatory time during the fiscal year 2009/2010

- The economic climate has not allowed budgetary flexibly for outsourcing. Though there is not a systematic process we do review contracts of outsourced service contracts to determine cost saving by in-sourcing. Example: Pest Control; the pest control contract was reviewed and a cost saving was identified by certifying employees' to provided this service. First year costs included training, certification and equipment for a cost of $6,479.62 vs. the outsourced fee of $19,712.55 for a first year saving of $13,232.93. Future saving projections are $18,439.53 per year.

- A two-pronged gang prevention strategy to combat gangs in Marion County was developed that focused on the reduction of criminal gang activity through law enforcement and community outreach programs. The strategy is federally grant funded and includes:

  - fulltime gang detective
  - community outreach basketball programs
  - identification of the most active gangs
  - creation of "gang track" software program, which allows tracking of gang members, associates and activities.
  - Targeted gang enforcement operations
  - Graffiti removal operation

The gang graffiti removal program is designed to eliminate "tagging" which identifies gang territory. Once a site is identified, an inmate work crew is sent to re-paint and clean the walls.

Graffiti Removal ↑ Good

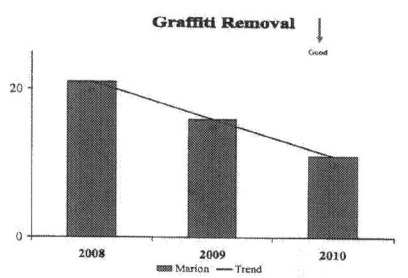

[Bar chart showing 2008, 2009, 2010 with downward trend]

Table PA 1.3

Strategic Adaptability

Provide two or three examples of opportunistic decision-making which led to strategic breakthroughs for the organization.

- An analysis of several facets of the Communications Center led to the discovery of areas needing improvement which were directly related to MCSO's guiding strategies; quality of service, and a safe and motivated workforce. These included:

  - Employee distribution did not align with peak times for calls for service.
  - During heavy call times, this meant calls were not being answered in the timely manner.
  - Employees were frustrated during heavy call times because of a lack of breaks and meal times.

APPENDIX B   129

Organizational Profile Addendum

- The schedule also required employees to frequently work on their days off.
- Due to the peak call loads, calls were not being answered in a timely manner.
- The facility itself was overcrowded and outdated.
- The phone system was outdated.
- An overload of activity on the police radio, which hampered the ability of deputies to communicate with dispatchers, thus creating a safety issue for deputies.

Solutions were developed as follows:
- A reallocation of manpower and a new schedule system was developed to align with peak calls for service.

- To more efficiently utilize existing manpower a "silent dispatch" work system was developed. This system utilizes the mobile data terminal (MDT) to communicate calls for service to deputies instead of verbally using the police radio. This allowed a reduction from three dispatch channels to two dispatch channels, thus freeing up dispatchers for breaks, meal times and also increase employees capability to keep scheduled days off. The reduction of radio traffic also increases the deputy's ability to get on the radio when needed. The ability of the deputies to create their own calls for service (security checks, case follow-ups, etc.) increased self initiated activity.

- A larger, state of the art Communication Center was constructed which is designed to withstand category 5 hurricanes. The facility includes break rooms, a tranquility room (to de-stress), exercise room. It also had a positive impact on employee issues such as noise levels, climate controls, 24-7 designed chairs, an overcrowded environment and a new automated phone answering system which distributes non emergency calls to other divisions.

- The Marion County Sheriff's Office Foundation, an approved 501(c)3 entity, was developed during the strategic planning process. The purpose is to supplement the financial burden associated with the activities of the many and varied volunteer groups that provide a direct benefit to the community and support the Sheriff's mission.

- In an effort to off-set the current economic downturn, MCSO elected to increase minor fee amounts for certain services; such as Records services, Inmate fees, and Civil Process fees. Florida State Statute authorizes the collection of fees for duplicating copies of public records. MCSO executed this innovation in October 2010. All monies collected will be treated as "unanticipated revenue" and remitted to the Board of County Commissioners to help counterbalance the current budget crisis.

The total increase in revenues and charges to be returned to the Board of County Commissioners for Fiscal Year 2010-2011 is estimated to be $514,615.

Criteria Changes

Criteria Changes

1.0 Leadership

1.1a(1); 1.1a(3) 1.2c; 1.2c(1)(2) 1.2(b)1

Marion County Sheriff's Office senior leaders promote the organization's core values with a commitment to community involvement. We support the customer's civic well-being through our direct involvement with local organizations, such as:

- United Way (Chairman)
- Salvation Army (Chairman of red kettle fundraising)
- Leadership Ocala/Marion (Board of Regents)
- Special Olympics (local coordinator)
- Southeastern Youth Fair (Executive board member)
- Harmony in the Streets (Summer day camp program for under privileged children. Includes a partnership with local schools and Florida Sheriff's Association.)
- Economic Development Council

The Marion County Sheriff's Office identifies twelve individual districts as its Key Communities. Each key community has regular crime watch meetings led by that specific district commander, affording us the opportunity to stay in touch with our communities' needs and concerns.

Senior leaders create a sustainable organization through the use of the strategic planning process, Quality Review Teams (QRT), Six Sigma process management, and an employee suggestion system. Organizational performance improvement is achieved through "STAT" processes. Employees are encouraged to pursue higher education through the college tuition reimbursement and step plan implementation. Senior leaders also nurture Line Level Supervisors by exposing them to the next level of supervision on a temporary basis as needed. This environment for organizational and workforce learning is key to succession planning. Senior leaders also participate in executive level learning such as Florida Department of Law Enforcement's Chief Executive Seminar and the Federal Bureau of Investigation National Academy.

The Marion County Sheriff's Office attempts to limit the impacts of our products on society as well as maintain good Stewardship to our customers. For example, in 2008, a strategic objective was initiated to reduce all utility consumption in the jail by 5% (CC Table 1.1). This goal was exceeded by removing unnecessary lighting, replacing existing T-12 light bulbs with energy efficient T-8 bulbs. Waterless urinals were installed in all male public and employee restrooms. This best practice was shared and implemented agency-wide. Timers were installed for inmate showers and toilets to reduce water consumption (CC Table 1.2).

A Solar Farm is in the installation phase which is projected to save $150,000 per year to heat water for the jail. The Inmate Work Farm provides beef, pork, chicken, eggs and vegetables to feed the inmates and staff at the jail. The by-product of

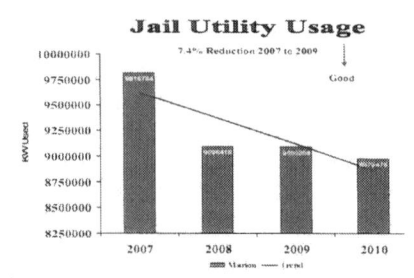

Jail Utility Usage

Table 1.1

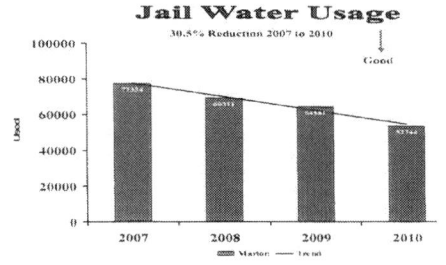

Jail Water Usage

Table 1.2

inmate meals (SWILL) is returned to the farm, heated by a wood burning stove, and fed to the pigs. The farm also utilizes chicken manure as fertilizer for the crops.

Regarding supply chain issues; efforts are made to reduce vehicle maintenance cost through a reduction in purchased parts. Vehicles taken out of service are placed in a surplus lot until every removable usable part has been redeployed. An auctioned surplus vehicle only yields approximately $2,500.00. Reutilizing parts returns approximately $7,000 per retired vehicle (CC Table 1.3).

1.2a(2)

This has been addressed in the original application.

Criteria Changes

Vehicle Maintenance Costs
34% Reduction 2007 to 2010

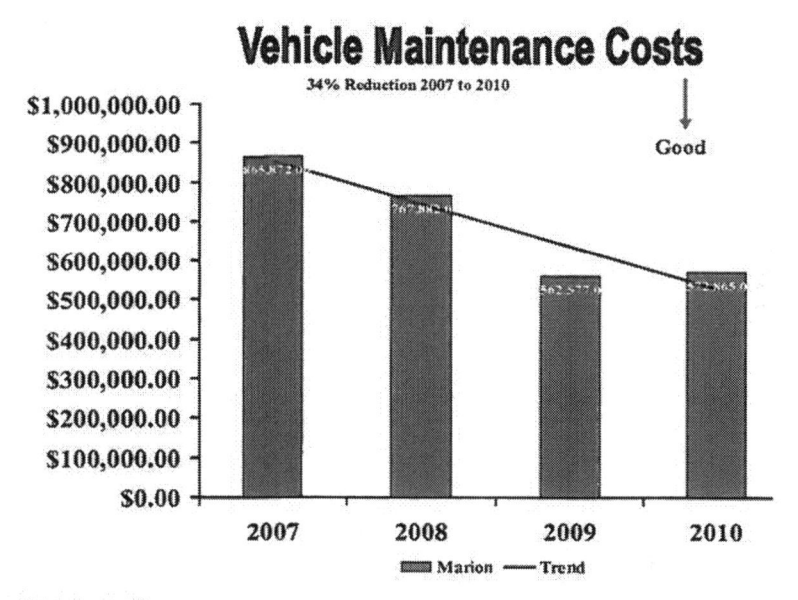

- 2007: $865,872.0
- 2008: $767,882.0
- 2009: $562,577.0
- 2010: $572,865.0 → Good

Marion —— Trend

Table 1.3

APPENDIX B 133

Criteria Changes

2.0 Strategic Planning

2.1a(1); 2.1a(2); 2.1b(2)

F.S.S. Chapter 30 and the Florida State Constitution dictates the duties of the Sheriff's Office. Strategic challenges and advantages are determined through our annual S.W.O.T. analysis, which begins at the line level and develops progressively through the senior staff level, to include participation of our volunteers, partners, and suppliers.

Longer term organizational sustainability is addressed through our multi-year plan which is structured similarly to our annual strategic plan (CC Table 2.1). Our multi-year plan has been used most recently to realize the new Emergency Operations Center, and the new Communications Center.

MCSO's Multi-year Plan is developed to guide the annual strategic plan for long term goals. This plan recognizes MCSO's guiding strategies Stewardship, Quality of Life, Safe and Motivated Workforce and Excellence of Service. The Multiyear Plan is reviewed annually and updated, as needed. It is intended to be a flexible document. Events and budgetary constraints can significantly alter prospective resources and timelines. The addition of a new Emergency Operations Center (EOC) and Communications Center provides the capability of meeting the needs of the community well into the future. These were built to accommodate unity of command among multiple first responder organizations.

The Sheriff's Office recently recommended that consolidation of the Marion County Fire Rescue Services under the auspices of the Sheriff's Office be explored. A blue ribbon panel was established by the Marion County Board of County Commissioners to explore this cost saving proposal. If approved, this will constitute a third core competency within the Sheriff's Office of Fire Rescue services.

2.2a(2)

Our workforce is informed of action steps through intra office bulletin board, e-mail, and shift briefings. Our volunteers, suppliers, partners, and collaborators are involved in the development of objectives by participation in the SWOT analysis and Senior Staff Strategic Planning Summit. The Strategic Plan is posted on the MCSO intranet and printable for each of the employees' action steps.

Criteria Changes

Guiding Strategies (Key Strategic Objectives)	Key Measures (Considered for Premier Status)	Key Measures					
		Actual/Target					
		10	11	12	13	14	15
Quality of Life	Part 1 Crime Rate per 1,000 Population	23 / 25	Target is to be at least one-half of the state-wide average				
	Part 1 Crime Clearance Rate 1,000 Population	53% / 44%	Target is to be at least twice the state average				
	Inmate Escapes	0 / 0	0	0	0	0	0
Stewardship	Law Enforcement Cost Per Capita	$168 / $196	For each year, the target is to be 30% below the "Best Florida Peer".				
	Inmate Cost Per Day	$47 / $49	$52	$55	$58	$62	$66
Safe and Motivated Work Force	Employee Retention	99.6% / 90%	To stay above 90%; this is above the U.S. Department of Labor standard of 80%.				
	Employee Satisfaction	67% / 80%	81%	82%	83%	84%	85%
	Average Workers Comp incidents per 100 employee	5 / 21	To have less than 21 Worker's Comp incidents per 100 employees, which is the average of the "Best Florida Peer".				
Excellence of Service	Overall Customer Satisfaction response	95% / 85%	To maintain 85% or greater, which exceeds the American Customer Satisfaction Index, which is currently 74%.				
	Overall satisfied with response by MCSO	95% / 85%	To maintain 85% or greater, which exceeds the American Customer Satisfaction Index, which is currently 74%.				
	Overall Customer Satisfaction with the way their call was handled	92% / 85%	To maintain 85% or greater, which exceeds the American Customer Satisfaction Index, which is currently 74%.				

Table 2.1

Criteria Changes

3.0 Customer and Market Focus

3.1a(2)

We encourage our customers to seek information, and conduct business with us through various listening posts. Our resources are available to the customer through the main operations building, communications center, jail information and visitation building, district offices, Public Information Officer and the web site. Interpreters are available for the non-English speaking customers. Commonly used forms and documentation are printed in both Spanish and English. Supervisor customer satisfaction surveys, district customer satisfaction surveys, inmate welfare line, 911 texting, and online reporting have all been implemented to encourage a consistently positive customer experience, and encourage customer engagement. Feedback from these interactions is reviewed during quarterly stat meetings, by the senior staff.

The "stat" processes provide a level of accountability to link the workforce performance management system to customer requirements.

New customers are acquired as the county population rises. The five (5) key customer requirements in Table P.1.6 are validated each year through our district offices, customer focus groups. All employees are provided "Sterling Wheel of Progress" cards that enable quick reference to the key customer requirements.

MCSO has implemented two (2) new programs to enhance customer follow-up. For the Law Enforcement core competency, a patrol sergeant survey was implemented in which a sergeant randomly surveys customers soon after a deputy provided them with service. For the Corrections core competency, an Inmate Welfare Line was implemented allowing customers to voice their concerns and check the well-being of inmates. This can be done either by phone or through the MSCO web site (email). These concerns are answered by a Watch Commander within 24 hours.

A citizen may file a complaint with any employee of the agency. A valid complaint is defined as one that is founded in fact with regard to an unacceptable personnel action or policy failure. Customer dissatisfaction is minimized by prompt resolution and feedback with any given complaint. All complaints will be fully investigated by a supervisor. If the complaint has been determined to be founded in fact and is in regards to a personnel action or policy failure, it is entered into the "Green Team" computer complaint tracking program. This program utilizes information to determine complaints about employees. Additionally, the "Green Team" software may identify employees who have had continuous complaints brought against them, as an early warning system.

A review of district level crime rate measurements led to the development of the High Intensity Patrol (H.I.P.) program to address customer concerns of crime in their neighborhoods. As a result of this, increased patrol activities resulted in crime reduction (CC Table 3.1).

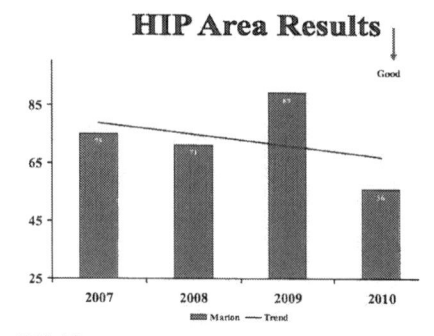

HIP Area Results

Table 3.1

Regular feedback from listening posts and examination of crime trends help MCSO identify and respond to customers needs. Examples of segmented customer services include:

- The Seniors At Risk Assistance Program which is designed specifically for senior citizens.

- Sex Offender Notification Program is designed to inform neighborhoods of the offenders residence.

- The inmate release process was streamlined due to concerns voiced by inmate's families.

Criteria Changes

4.0 Measurement, Analysis and Knowledge Management

4.1a(1); 4.1c
The changes in this section were addressed in 4.1 a (1) – question 2 and 4.1 b (2) – question 3 on the original application.

5.0 Workforce Focus

5.1a(3); 5.1b1; 5.2(a)3 and 5.2b(1)
Has been addressed in the original application. Additions to 5.2 b (1) have been made in the response to the O.F.I. document.

Criteria Changes

6.0 Process Management

6.1a(2)
MCSO's work systems continue to be designed around the two core competencies, law enforcement and corrections. Since the GSA, we have streamlined the organization and now there are four divisions.

Table 6.1.1 Core Competencies, Key Process, Measures

Core Competencies	Key Work Process	Key Process Requirement(s)	Key Performance Measure(s)
Law Enforcement	Community Policing Department	• Crime prevention • Solve crimes • Manage volunteers • Respond citizens concerns • Community education and awareness • Manage volunteers	• Part 1 Crime rate per 1,000 (Figure 7.1.1) • Part 1 Crime clearance rate (Figure 7.1.2) • Total Volunteer valued effort (Figure 7.3.6) • Number of Self-initiated activities (Figure 7.5.1) • Average Response times (Figure 7.1.5) • Overall Customer Satisfied Response (Figure 7.2.1) • Overall Customer Satisfied Way Call Handled (Figure 7.2.2)
	Special Investigation Department	• Solve crime • Process DNA • Respond citizens concerns • Narcotics/vice investigations • Respond citizens concerns	• Part 1 Crime clearance rate (Figure 7.1.2) • DNA measure cycle time (Figure 7.5.2) • Overall Customer Satisfied Response (Figure 7.2.1) • Overall Customer Satisfied Way Call Handled (Figure 7.2.2) • Part 1 Crime rate per 1,000 (Figure 7.1.1) • Part 1 Crime clearance rate (Figure 7.1.2) • Total Tips closed (Figure 7.5.3) • Percentage of UDEST goals achieved (Figure 7.5.5) • Overall Customer Satisfied Response (Figure 7.2.1) • Overall Customer Satisfied Way Call Handled (Figure 7.2.2)
	Corrections Department – Civil	• Serve subpoenas • Serve Protective Orders	• Percent of Writs Successfully Served (Figure 7.5.10) • Percent Protective Orders attempted within 24 hours (Figure 7.5.11)
Corrections	Corrections Department	• Custody & Security • Cost effective • Custody of inmates during court proceedings • WILA	• Number Escapes from Jail or Transport (Figure 7.1.3) • Inmate Cost Per Day (Figure 7.3.2) • Use of Force per 100 inmates (Figure 7.5.9) • Accreditation Florida Model Jail Standards (Figure 7.6.9) • Number of Escapes from court proceedings (Figure 7.5.12) • Juvenile programs success rate (Figure 7.5.7)

6.1b(1)
Streamlining the organization has included cost reductions promoting stewardship and providing cost savings to the customers with an emphasis on minimal reduction in services to the customer. Since FY '07-'08 MCSO has experienced a 6% reduction in budget while continuing to maintain strong performance levels as reflected in Category 7 results.

6.2b(2)
MCSO uses a Rapid Process Improvement tool (R.P.I.) from the Six Sigma philosophy and the Quality Review Teams (Q.R.T.) to analyze the work processes. These systematic processes include recommendations for implementation of changes or new programs. Examples include:

- An RPI was conducted on the criminal subpoena process and we were able to eliminate one person from the process, thus saving man hours which could be utilized in other work areas.

- An RPI was conducted on the Crime Stoppers process. It was determined that there was rework in several of the steps and there were duplicated services which were eliminated; allowing the employees to utilize their time in other work areas and providing more timely transfer of information.

Criteria Changes

6.2c

Organizational performance review results are systematically evaluated during the quarterly "stat" process. For example, during Communications stat (COMSTAT), response times were analyzed and a solution to reduce response times was formulated. Dispatchers are required to notify a sergeant if a call is pending more than 10 minutes and they are required to notify

Key Work Support Processes	Key Process Requirements	Key Performance Measure(s)
Fleet Maintenance	Timely repair of vehicles	• Fleet Maintenance Turn Around Time (Figure 7.5.13)
Human Resource	Filling vacant positions	• % Vacancy Rating (Figure 7.5.14)
	Manage benefits	• % Employee Retention (Figure 7.4.6)
Fiscal Management	Manage budget	• Number of "written" comments (Figure 7.6.4)
	Prompt payment invoices	• Percent of Invoices paid within 45 day (Figure 7.5.15)
Information & Technology	Computer system maintenance	• System up time (Figure 7.5.16)
Training	Provide training & development	• Compliance FDLE Training Requirements (Figure 7.6.7) • Employee satisfaction training (Figure 7.4.11) • Training effectiveness (Figure 7.4.10)
Key Suppliers	**Key Process Requirement(s)**	**Key Performance Measure(s)**
Ocala Community Care	Provide cost efficient medical care	Medical costs per ADP (Figure 7.3.9)
Key Partners	**Key Process Requirement(s)**	**Key Performance Measure(s)**
MADET/ HIDTA	Drug enforcement	Percentage of UDEST goals achieved (Figure 7.5.5)
FDLE	DNA	DNA Screening Turn-Around Time (Figure 7.5.2)

Table 6.1.3, Key Support Processes, Suppliers, Partners

a watch commander if a call is pending more than 20 minutes. This solution was shared during the Operations Stat (OPSTAT) and District statistics (DSTAT) and implemented. As a result, response times have decreased. (Figure 7.1.5)

Senior leaders become the conduit between the stat processes. For example, to support the Law Enforcement core competency, information shared during the OPS stat process for the Watch Commanders is shared with the District Commanders during the DSTAT process through the senior leadership.

Information sharing occurs during the stat meetings as well as senior staff meetings. For example, This led to the discovery of an available grant for the Rapid I.D. system, which is a portable fingerprint scanning system used to identify suspects in the field. This technology was originally applied to the Law Enforcement group. This information was determined to also be useful in the Corrections group to facilitate a more rapid identification of offenders that draws from a larger data base.

Opportunities for Improvement

Opportunities for Improvement

1.0 Leadership

1.1b(2)
Senior leaders focus on the alignment of break though improvement and innovation to overcome the economic challenges to maintain a premier status. For example, when it was necessary to decrease the budget by $3.2 million, MCSO assumed the responsibility of care, custody and control of juveniles from the State of Florida's Division of Juvenile Justice (DJJ). This innovative response saved Marion County taxpayers $3.2 million, budgeted to the state for this role. Innovations such as this improve performance and attain the organization's vision to maintain premier status.

1.2a (2)
During the quarterly meeting with QRT members their presentation, organization, and communication skills are improved and reinforced. This is a positive improvement process that identifies and nurtures future leaders' potential.

Opportunities for Improvement

2.0 Strategic Planning

2.1a(2)
After review of our process, it was found that MCSO analyzes all relevant data and information pertaining to the strategic planning process. SWOT analysis begins at the line level and progresses upward through the chain of command. MCSO analyzes relevant data to identify potential blind spots and customer needs and this is accomplished through the "stat" process. Division Stat reviews are where strategic challenges and breakthrough improvements are analyzed. MCSO feels this is a systematic process that enables us to continue as a premier, valued centered Sheriff's Office. Our active participation with customer "Listening Posts" as described in the original GSA application provides another systematic process to identify potential blind spots and customer needs.

2.2a(4)
MCSO has reviewed its longer-term action steps for longer-term strategic planning, including capital improvement projects and found that MCSO shows a systematic approach to longer-term action plans. For example, the Emergency Operations Center development plan included objectives and action steps from 2006 through 2009. The 911 Communications Center phase was started in 2008 and completed in 2010 with objectives and action steps in each year's plan. Both improvements meet the key measures of Quantity of Life, Stewardship, Safe and Motivated Workforce, and Excellence of Service.

2.2b
MCSO considers the targets listed in the key performance measures as performance projections (P.1.2). In addition, examples of "foresight" would include the following:

- Due to up-coming budget restraints, MCSO was tasked at looking at possibilities for savings. In November 2010 this became a reality, with the transfer of responsibility from the Department of Juvenile Justice to the Marion County Sheriff's Office for housing juveniles at the Marion County Jail (PA-Recent Improvements) We are the first law enforcement agency to have the "foresight" on this topic and currently other agencies are looking at MCSO's juvenile model for cost saving and functionality. This function will save the taxpayers millions of dollars each year. Another example is "911 texting." We are the only law enforcement agency in the United States with this capability. MCSO's "foresight" led to this innovation and new level of customer service. This software was developed in-house by our I.T. department. This is a growing need to provide additional options for the citizens to reach emergency services.

2.2b
Table 2.1.1 identifies projected targets and goals in line with our Guiding Strategies. For example, MCSO's target is to clear 50% of our part one crimes (Figure 7.1.1, 7.1.2), which translates to twice the state average; constituting role model performance. MCSO's "Best Florida Peers" do not provide projected performance goals. Progress is ensured through our strategic plan and the accountability through our stat processes.

Opportunities for Improvement

3.0 Customer and Market Focus

3.1a(1), 3.2a (4) & 3.2b (4)
MCSO has implemented a supervisor survey instrument, District level surveys, Jail surveys and High Intensity Patrol (HIP) areas. For example, Supervisor surveys are conducted randomly throughout the month. A citizen from the specific district for which the deputy works is called and surveyed after the deputy has completed their call for service; giving MCSO immediate feedback on the deputies' and the Agency's performance. Another example of an improved segmented customer focus response is the improved HIP area program which is a new system. Crime trends are analyzed to determine areas with upward crime trends. Once a HIP area is determined, it is reinforced with up-scaled patrol and in some cases, more deputies' are assigned to that specific area to deter crime and conduct pro-active measures. An example of the success of this program was a 37% reduction in crime in the North West District (CC-Table 3.1).

3.1a(4)
As stated in the response in 3.1.a1 MCSO modified the customer survey instrument and process and created a new listening post through the sergeant's survey method.

Opportunities for Improvement

4.0 Measurement, Analysis and Knowledge Management

4.1a (2)
MCSO looks at other organizations and performance to determine benchmarks as needed. For example, problems with the previously contracted inmate health-care provider led to research of their performance in Florida as well as other areas of the United States. The OCC innovation for inmate health care at MCSO was modeled from a nationally recognized program being used in Hampden County, Massachusetts.

4.1b (1)
MCSO has implemented the rapid process improvement system. Listed below are RPI's that have been conducted since 2008.

RPI's
- Warrants Unit – Validations
- Property Disposals
- Inmate Release Process
- Inmate Control Room Process
- First Appearance
- Seniors At Risk Assistance; SARA Program
- Work In Lieu of Arrest; WILA Program
- Graffiti Removal Process
- Money Forfeiture Accountability Stream
- P.C. Affidavit Approval Process
- Crime Stoppers
- Intoxilyzer/DUI Arrest Processes

4.2a(3)
MCSO has moved the main data servers for the agency into the new Communications Center. This building is hardened to withstand a category five hurricane. MCSO continues to perform Storage Area Network (SAN) by backing up the data and storing it in a bunker located at the jail.

4.2b(2)
MCSO shares best practices at weekly Senior Staff meetings. All divisions within the agency are represented at this weekly meeting. Best Practices are shared at that time with all division heads and also shared with line level employees as listed below:

- The activities of Quality Review Teams are listed on MCSO Share Point for the whole agency to review.
- The Quality Review Team leaders meet quarterly for sharing purposes.
- Employee suggestion Box is accessible on MCSO Share Point and monitored daily.
- Monthly MCSO Gazette "newsletter" distributed electronically Agency wide.

Opportunities for Improvement

| 5.0 Workforce Focus |

5.1c(2)
Employee satisfaction surveys are reviewed and analyzed by Division Heads to determine areas needing improvement: For example, in the Communications Center, it was determined morale was being influenced by schedules and the stressful environment of the position. Schedules were evaluated and a more innovative approach to scheduling was implemented, which was to stagger shifts at peek call load times. A new work process was implemented, streamlining the radio functions which allowed dispatchers to receive breaks on a regular basis. The new Communications Center was built with a tranquility room for operators/dispatchers to de-stress after a critical call or extremely high call volume (PA-Opportunistic Decision-making).

5.2b(1)
MCSO reviews all Worker Compensation incidents to determine a pattern/trend to correct the problem. MCSO is also inspected quarterly by the Hunt Insurance Group, which is MCSO's workers compensation insurer. An on site inspection is conducted facility wide and includes a written summary of their findings and recommendations. To date, there have been no shortcomings or recommendations. The Corrections Division assigns a Fire, Safety, Security and Sanitation Officer to conduct systematic inspections on a weekly basis. Since 2008 these process have contributed to a 35.5% reduction rate in workers compensation incidents. (Figure 7.4.8)

Opportunities for Improvement

| 6.0 Process Management |

6.1a(1)
MCSO's proactive approach included attending community meetings in neighborhoods being considered for annexation. Those communities voted against annexation and the annexation push has subsided. MCSO promotes new ideas and innovations throughout the listening posts. In addition, the agency has a proactive policy of discussing significant improvement ideas with the Sheriff's Advisory Council and the Editorial Board of the local newspaper. There have been several editorials lauding the innovative efforts of the Sheriff's Office.

6.2b
MCSO currently reviews processes by utilizing the RPI tool from the Six Sigma system and Quality Review Teams to analyze and improve work processes (4.1.b(1)).

Opportunities for Improvement

7.0 Results

7.1a
The following outcome measures are segmented internally to address customer groups. One example is at the district level.
- 7.1.1 Part One Crime Rate Per 1,000 Citizens
- 7.1.2 Part One Crime Clearance Rate
- 7.1.5 Response Time
- 7.1.6 Over all Customer Satisfaction

7.2a
The survey instrument has been adjusted to measure visibility, problem solving, and communication. The data is also segmented internally.

7.3a
Benchmarking and comparisons are difficult because of the differences in how other law enforcement/corrections agencies operate. Some examples of these differences include:
- manpower allocation
- millage rates for funding
- program offerings
- population, demographic, geographic and density variances.

7.4a(3)
The use of sick leave per 1000 hours worked continues to fluctuate on a consistent scale.

7.4a
This data is not tracked

7.5a
Some of these measures are unique to MCSO so no comparisons have been identified. The remaining data for comparisons is not tracked.

7.6a(4)
Energy conservation has been tracked with improvements made. (CC- 1.2(b)1)

APPENDIX B   147

Organizational Performance Results

7.1 Product & Performance Outcomes

One of the core competencies of the Sheriff's Office is law enforcement. Law enforcement key indicators are measured through an in-depth review of crime trending. Listening posts provide information on how to better serve the community and our pro-active crime prevention programs help to stop crimes before they are committed. Trending of this information is imperative in understanding when and where crimes occur the most and where resources need to be allocated. This information is then compared to our "Best Florida Peers" and prior GSA recipients to ensure we are providing the best product to the citizens of Marion County.

Corrections, which oversees the operation of the Marion County Jail, is another core competency of the Marion County Sheriff's Office. Corrections includes key support processes such as custody and security, food service, inmate programs, medical, Bailiff services, and others. Corrections key indicators are measured by various analyses of data. This information is also compared to our "Best Florida Peers" to ensure we are providing the best product to the citizens of Marion County.

Part 1 Crime Rate Per 1000 Citizens

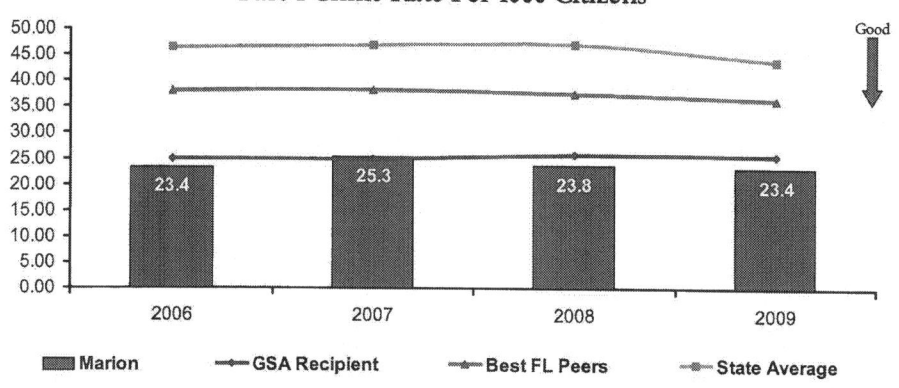

Year	Marion
2006	23.4
2007	25.3
2008	23.8
2009	23.4

Legend: Marion, GSA Recipient, Best FL Peers, State Average

Figure 7.1.1 compares the Part 1 Crime Rate against our "Best Florida Peers". Part 1 crimes include murder, rape, robbery, aggravated assault, burglary, larceny, and theft.

Part 1 Crime Clearance Rate

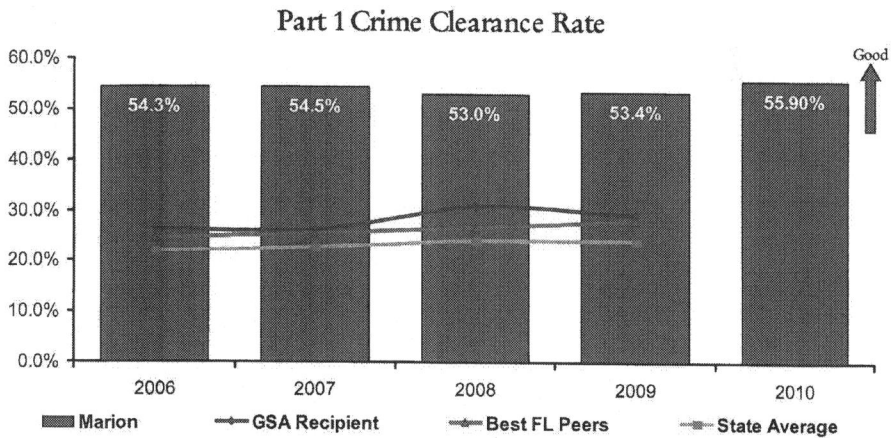

Year	Marion
2006	54.3%
2007	54.5%
2008	53.0%
2009	53.4%
2010	55.90%

Legend: Marion, GSA Recipient, Best FL Peers, State Average

Figure 7.1.2 compares the Part 1 Crime Clearance Rate against our "Best Florida Peers". Part 1 crimes include murder, rape, robbery, aggravated assault, burglary, larceny, and theft.

Number of Escapes from Jail — Good ↓

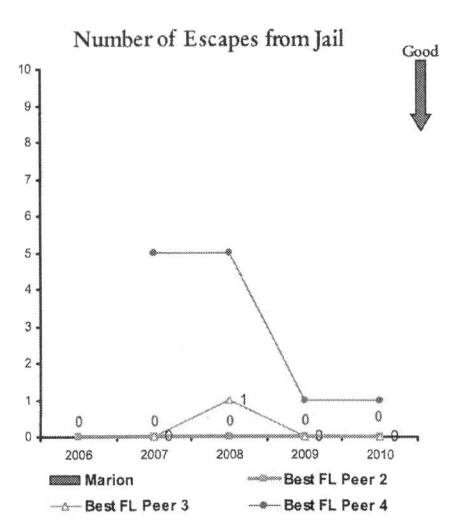

Figure 7.1.3 compares the number of escapes from the jail to our "Best Florida Peers." There have been no successful escapes from the Marion County jail since 1989.

Inmate to Inmate Batteries Per 1,000 — Good ↓

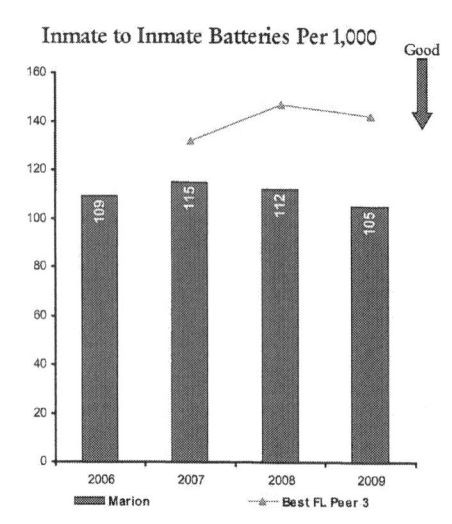

Marion: 109 (2006), 115 (2007), 112 (2008), 105 (2009)

Figure 7.1.4 compares inmate to inmate batteries.

Average Response Time — Good ↓

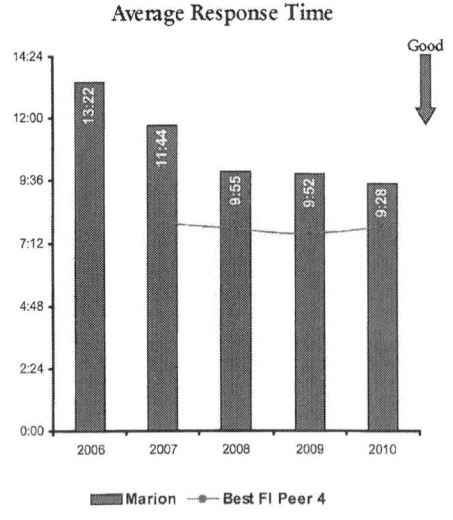

Marion: 13:22 (2006), 11:44 (2007), 9:55 (2008), 9:52 (2009), 9:28 (2010)

Figure 7.1.5 compares the average response time from received to arrived, which is a key customer requirement.

Overall Customer Satisfaction — Good ↑

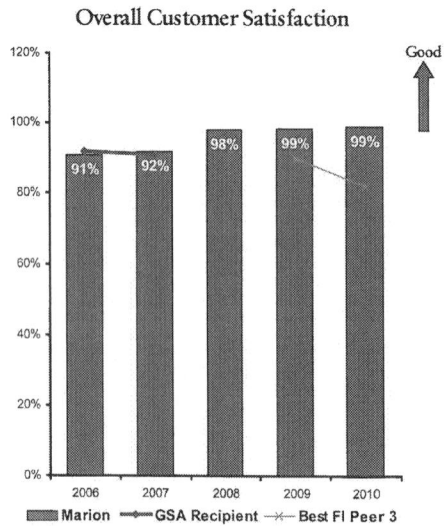

Marion: 91% (2006), 92% (2007), 98% (2008), 99% (2009), 99% (2010)

Figure 7.1.6 compares the overall customer satisfaction.

7.2 Customer Focused Outcomes

The Marion County Sheriff's Office has chosen American Customer Satisfaction Index (ACSI) Government Survey Results and our Best Florida Peers to provide the benchmark for Customer and Market knowledge comparable data. The Marion County Sheriff's Office collects data in the following areas and measures the results: "The Employee Was Professional and Helpful," "The Customer Was Overall Satisfied With The Way The Call Was Handled," "The Deputy Responded In A Reasonable Time," and "The Customer Was Satisfied With The Response By The Sheriff's Office."

Overall Satisfied With Response By S.O.

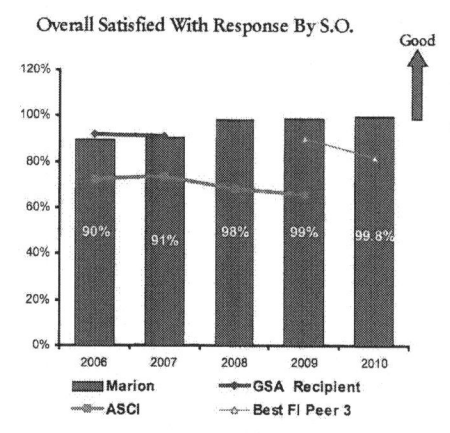

Year	Marion
2006	90%
2007	91%
2008	98%
2009	99%
2010	99.8%

Figure 7.2.1 compares overall customer satisfaction with the Sheriff's Office Response.

Overall Satisfied With The Way Call Was Handled

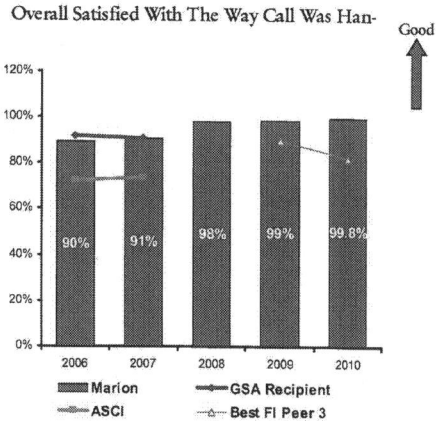

Year	Marion
2006	90%
2007	91%
2008	98%
2009	99%
2010	99.8%

Figure 7.2.2 compares overall customer satisfaction with the way the call for service was handled.

The Employee was Professional and Helpful

Year	Marion
2006	94%
2007	95%
2008	98%
2009	99%
2010	99.7%

Figure 7.2.3 indicates that the Sheriff's Office employees are professional and helpful.

They Responded in a Reasonable Time

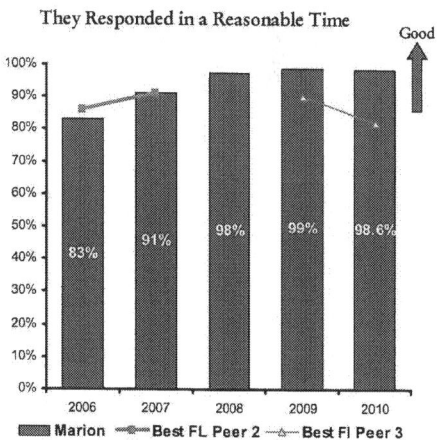

Year	Marion
2006	83%
2007	91%
2008	98%
2009	99%
2010	98.6%

Figure 7.2.4 indicates that the Sheriff's Office responds to the needs of the citizens in a timely manner.

7.3 Financial and Market Outcomes

An important part of stewardship is to ensure our customers receive the best of each tax dollar entrusted to the Sheriff's Office. This is monitored by budgets, comparisons to other law enforcement agencies, management of resources, and other financial activity measures. Eight out of every ten citizens in Marion County fall under the jurisdiction of the Marion County Sheriff's Office.

Law Enforcement Cost Per Capita

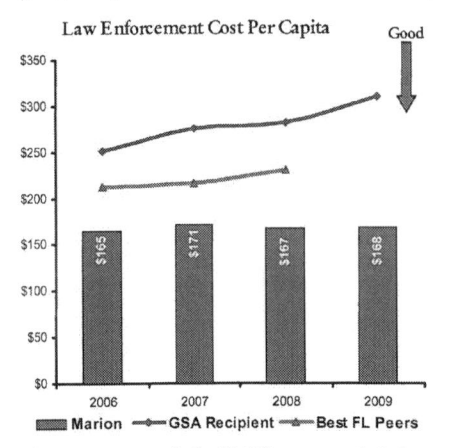

Figure 7.3.1 compares the Sheriff's Office cost per capita for law enforcement services to the "Best Florida Peers" and a GSA Recipient.

Inmate Average Cost Per Day

Figure 7.3.2 compares the Sheriff's Office average inmate cost per day to the "Best Florida Peers."

Percentage of Fiscal Year Funds Expended

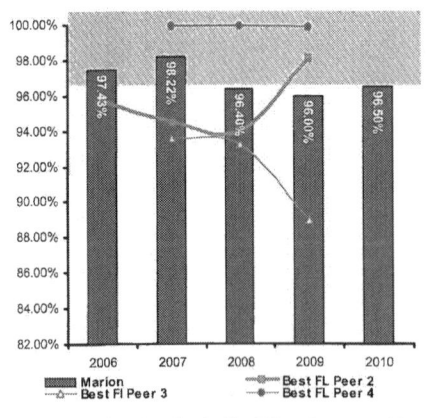

Figure 7.3.3 shows how the Sheriff's Office strives to spend its resources frugally. Our target is 96-100%, and any excess funds are returned to the County. This is accomplished by monitoring execution of the budget during monthly meetings with the Sheriff and his Senior Staff.

Sworn Law Enforcement vs. Non-Sworn

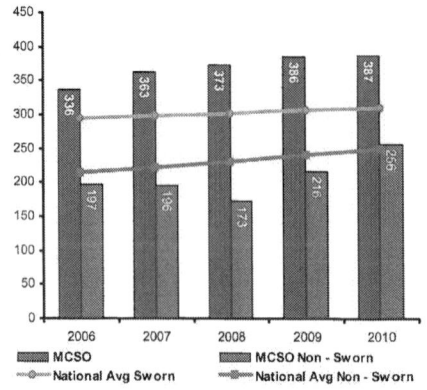

Figure 7.3.4. MCSO continues to maintain high levels of customer service by adding additional sworn personnel over time, but maintaining stewardship. MCSO accomplishes this by maintaining an appropriate level of non-sworn support personnel. Since 2006, MCSO has increased Patrol Deputy and Sergeants responsible for calls for service by 15%.

152 SERVANT GOVERNING

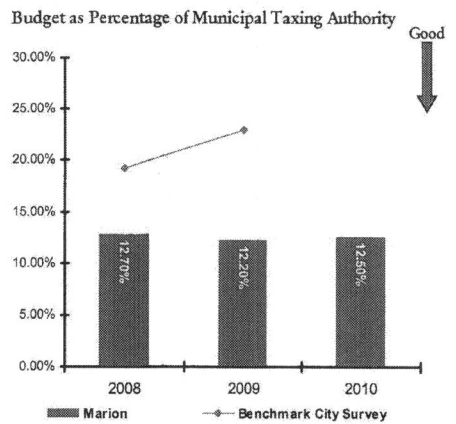

Budget as Percentage of Municipal Taxing Authority

Figure 7.3.5. The Sheriff's Office recognizes its responsibility to the citizens of Marion County. As a percentage of total Municipal/County taxing authority, MCSO has averaged around 12.47% for the past three years, as compared to a national benchmark city survey.

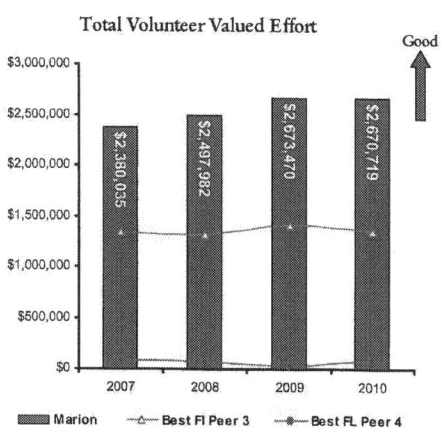

Total Volunteer Valued Effort

Figure 7.3.6 compares the yearly savings by including volunteers. The value of volunteer time is based on the average hourly earnings of all production and non-supervisory workers on private non-farm payrolls (as determined by the Bureau of Labor Statistics).

Jail to Work Program

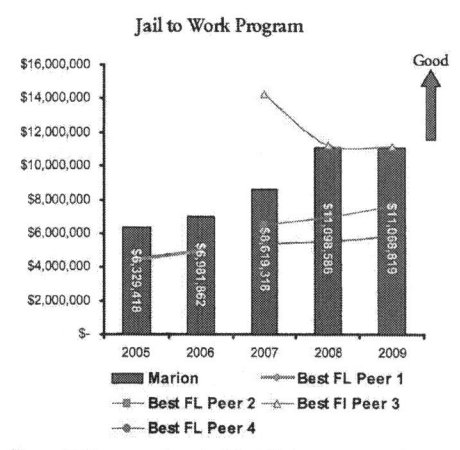

Figure 7.3.7 compares how the Jail to Work program provides a value to stakeholders by utilizing inmate labor (based on minimum wage) to keep cost per day low. This program also helps manage other costs around the county such as facility maintenance with parks, fire stations, etc.

Value of Inmate Work Farm

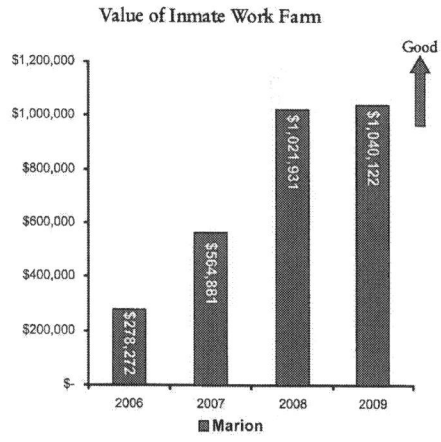

Figure 7.3.8 compares the dollar value of commodities yielded at the inmate work farm. This directly contributes to the inmate average cost per day. Our Best Florida Peers do not have a work farm to compare data.

APPENDIX B 153

Yearly Medical Cost Per Average Inmate Population

	2007	2008	2009
Marion	$2,955	$3,338	$3,907
DOC	$4,336	$4,752	$5,184

Good ↓

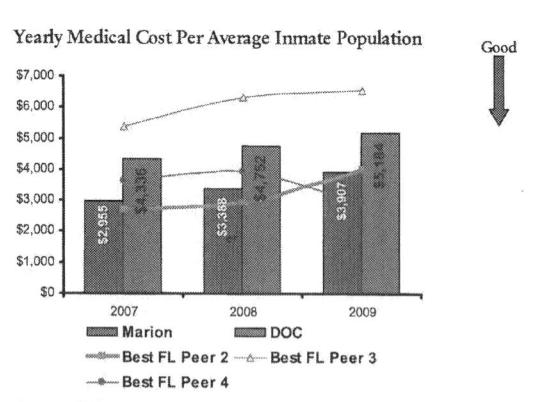

Figure 7.3.9 compares yearly medical cost per average inmate population.

7.4 Human Resource Outcomes

MCSO supports high performance through an employee award system and employee performance appraisal and measurement system. Learning and development is encouraged through the higher education reimbursement program. Additionally, management and leadership development is fostered by an opportunity for all management level employees to attend Command School.

Indicators of employee well-being and satisfaction are employee retention and employee survey results. "Best Florida Peers" do not conduct employee surveys, therefore data is unavailable. However, as appropriate, comparisons are made against former GSA recipients where available and the Federal Human Capital Survey.

Employee Satisfaction

Year	Marion	GSA Recipient
2006	75%	
2007	84%	
2008	85%	
2010	64%	

Good ↑

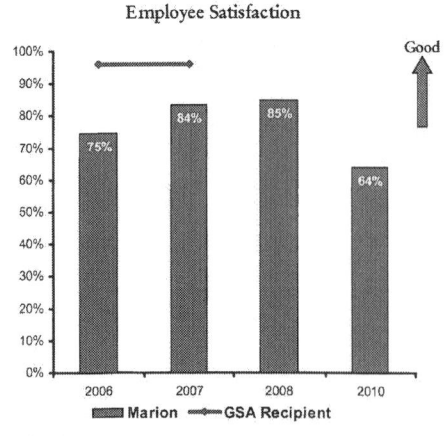

Figure 7.4.1. The organization conducts employee surveys to determine overall employee satisfaction and customer service.

I Am Satisfied With My Job

Year	Marion	Federal Human Capital Survey
2006	82%	
2007	88%	
2008	89%	
2010	76%	

Good ↑

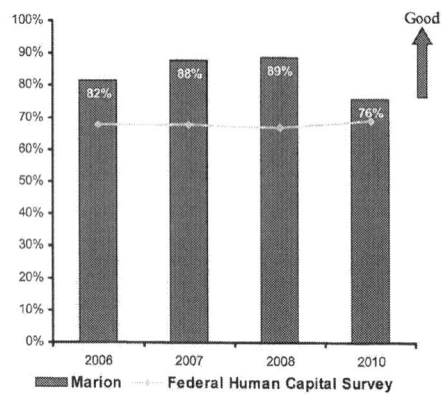

Figure 7.4.2 reflects employees satisfaction with employment at the Sheriff's Office.

Encourage Development of Job Skills So I Can Advance

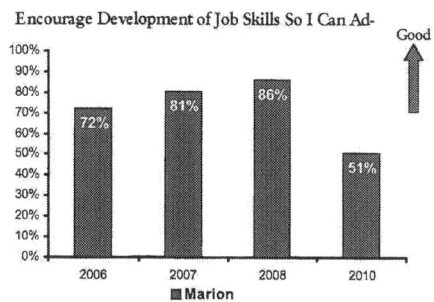

Marion: 2006: 72%, 2007: 81%, 2008: 86%, 2010: 51%

Figure 7.4.3. The Sheriff's Office encourages job skills development through mentoring and the evaluation process. All supervisors holding the rank of sergeant or above are required to attend leadership/management development school. Education is encouraged at all levels of the organization.

Employee Tools and Equipment

Marion: 2006: 60%, 2007: 80%, 2008: 80%, 2010: 60%

Figure 7.4.4. As indicated in the Employee Survey, the Sheriff's Office employees are polled as to the necessary tools and equipment to carry out their duties.

Workforce Reflects Community

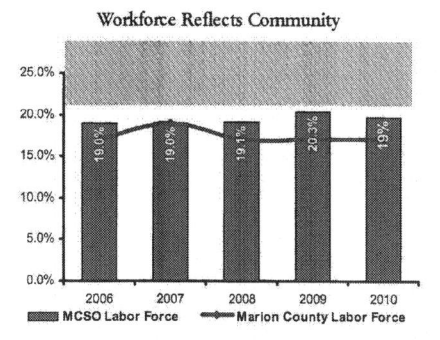

MCSO Labor Force: 2006: 19.0%, 2007: 19.0%, 2008: 19.1%, 2009: 20.3%, 2010: 19%
— Marion County Labor Force

Figure 7.4.5. The Sheriff's Office workforce is compared to available Marion County minority workforce.

Employee Retention

Marion: 2006: 92.0%, 2007: 94.0%, 2008: 95%, 2009: 95.6%, 2010: 94.5%

Figure 7.4.6 indicates the employee retention rate for the Sheriff's Office.

Sick Leave Per 1,000 Hours Worked

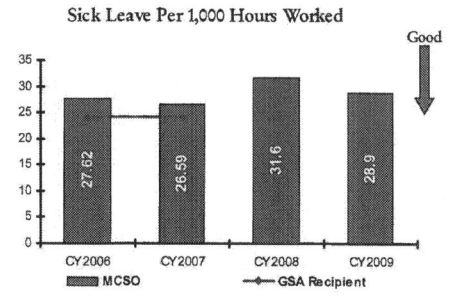

MCSO: CY2006: 27.62, CY2007: 26.59, CY2008: 31.6, CY2009: 28.9
— GSA Recipient

Figure 7.4.7. This chart reflects the net sick leave usage, excluding another employee benefit for DROP Sick leave pay outs.

Workers Compensation Incidents Per 100

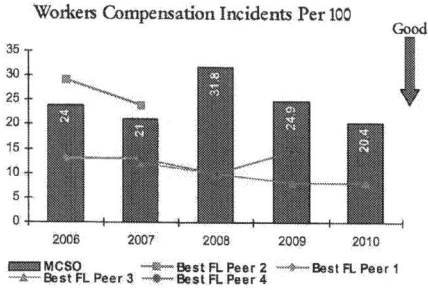

MCSO: 2006: 24, 2007: 21, 2008: 31.8, 2009: 24.9, 2010: 20.4
Best FL Peer 1, Best FL Peer 2, Best FL Peer 3, Best FL Peer 4

Figure 7.4.8. Workers compensation incidents are an indicator of a safe and motivated workforce.

APPENDIX B 155

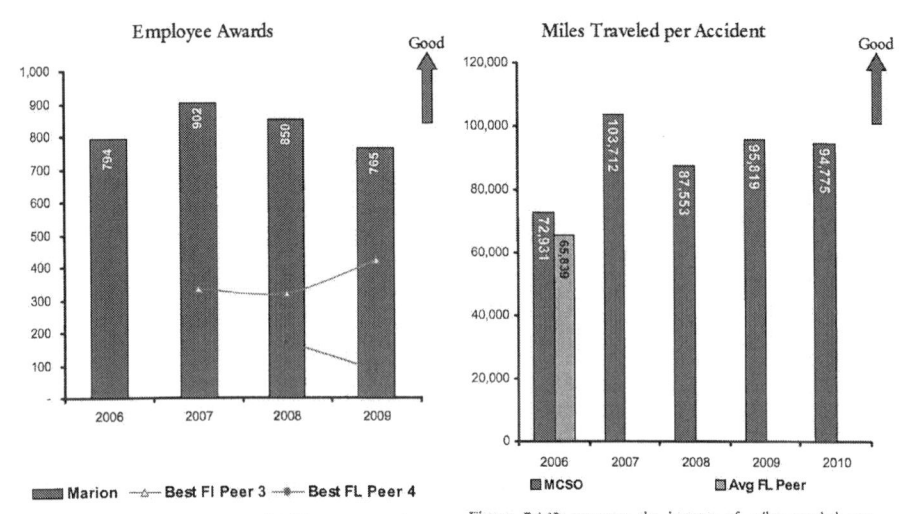

Figure 7.4.9. The Marion County Sheriff's Office recognizing the employees for their achievements.

Figure 7.4.10 compares the increase of miles traveled per accident as a measure of training effectiveness. Our "Best Florida Peers" did not provide current comparative data.

Figure 7.4.11. The Sheriff's Office conducts and provides training opportunities on a continuous basis.

7.5 Organizational Effectiveness Outcomes

The strategic planning process identifies the agency strategic objectives and develops a guide to strategic challenges. Through leadership meetings and by soliciting input from line personnel, strengths, weaknesses, opportunities and threats are identified. Ongoing research keeps the agency abreast of changes and developments in applicable technologies, law, and the needs of the community. Strategic objectives are periodically reviewed to help determine how well the agency is meeting the needs of key stake holders. The effectiveness of strategic planning and the programs implemented through strategic planning are measured on a continuing basis in a series of "stat meetings".

Each division has quarterly stat meetings in which supervisors present reports on the performance of the area under their supervision for the previous quarter. Annual cumulative data are included in the quarterly reports to track the year-to-date results and summarize how each area is performing with respect to the strategic plan. In addition to reporting the year-to-date and previous quarter results, each supervisor gives a projection of what adjustments need to be made to stay on track. The stat reports keep the Division Head apprised of the overall performance of each division so that senior staff can make adjustments to keep the entire organization aligned with the strategic plan.

Number of Self-Initiated Activities

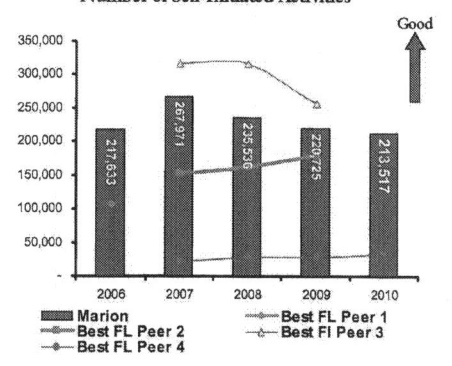

Figure 7.5.1 compares the number of self-initiated activity conducted by all deputies each year. Self-initiated activities are categorized as any proactive duties performed by deputies, such as traffic stops, security checks, neighborhood watch, citizen contacts, etc.

DNA Screening Average Turn-Around Time in Days

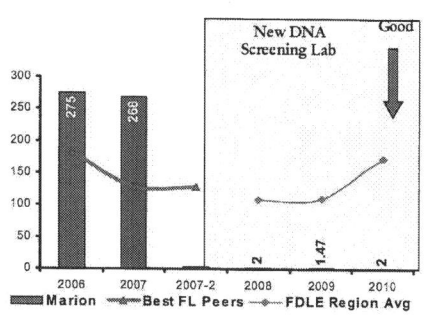

Figure 7.5.2 compares the Turn-Around Time in days for cases requiring screening at the FDLE Serology Lab by the Best Florida Peers compared to MCSO. Increasing DNA turnaround time helps solve crime and faster

Percentage of Tip Sheets Closed

Figure 7.5.3. When a tip sheet is received, it is reviewed by a supervisor and assigned to either the appropriate district or a drug agent for further investigation. There are times when a tip sheet requires a lengthy investigation and this may cause the tip sheet to remain open for an extended period of time.

Percentage of Cargo Theft Recoveries

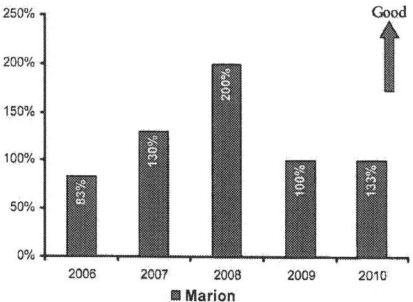

Figure 7.5.4 compares the recovery percentage of all commercial semi cargo tractors and/or trailers stolen in Marion County.

APPENDIX B **157**

Percentage of UDEST Goals Achieved

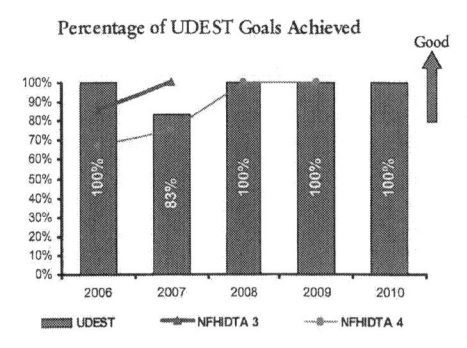

- 2006: 100% (UDEST)
- 2007: 83%
- 2008: 100%
- 2009: 100%
- 2010: 100%

Series: UDEST, NFHIDTA 3, NFHIDTA 4

Figure 7.5.5. The mission of UDEST is to disrupt and dismantle major drug trafficking organizations by identifying, arresting and prosecuting the individuals or networks responsible for the importation and distribution of drugs in Marion County.

Community Awareness Education Programs

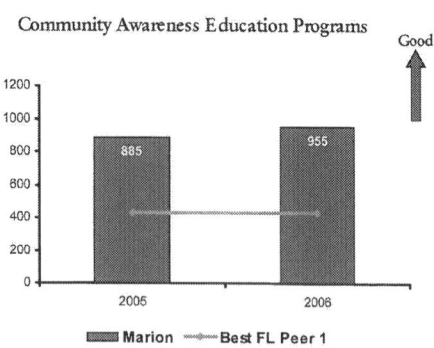

- 2005: 885
- 2006: 955

Series: Marion, Best FL Peer 1

Figure 7.5.6 Although we still provide numerous community awareness education programs, we no longer track this activity measure.

Juvenile Programs Completion Rate

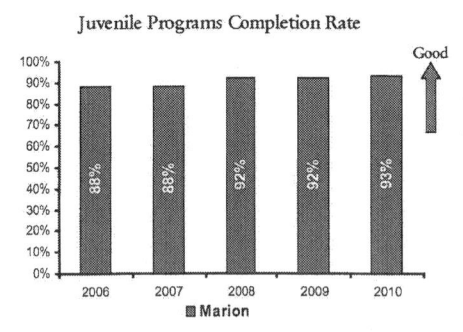

- 2006: 88%
- 2007: 88%
- 2008: 92%
- 2009: 92%
- 2010: 93%

Series: Marion

Figure 7.5.7 compares the completion rate of juvenile programs. Our Best Florida Peers have not responded with any comparable data.

Inmate to Officer Batteries Per 1,000 ADP

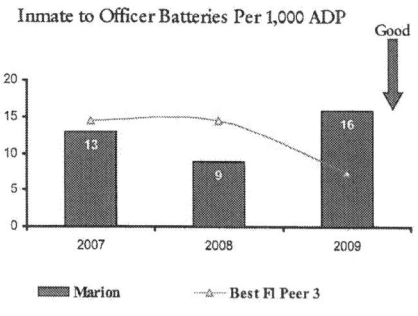

- 2007: 13
- 2008: 9
- 2009: 16

Series: Marion, Best Fl Peer 3

Figure 7.5.8 compares the inmate to officer batteries.

Use of Force Per 1,000 ADP

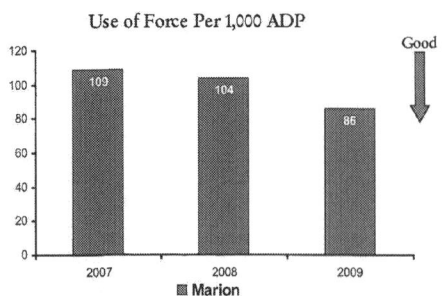

- 2007: 109
- 2008: 104
- 2009: 86

Series: Marion

Figure 7.5.9 shows the use of force per 1,000 ADP. "Best Florida Peers" data is not calculated the same as Marion County, therefore comparable data is not available.

Writs Successfully Served

- 2006: 84%
- 2007: 90%
- 2008: 88%
- 2009: 87%
- 2010: 86%

Series: Marion, Best FL Peer 1, Best FL Peer 2, Best FL Peer 3, Best FL Peer 4

Figure 7.5.10 compares the percentage of civil papers served within the necessary timeframe.

Protective Orders Attempted Within 24 Hours

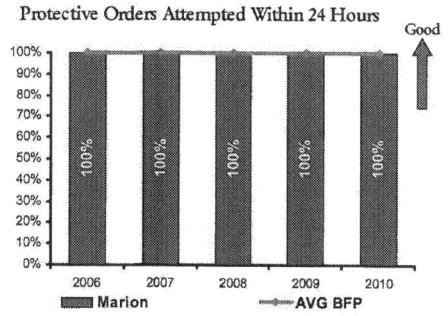

Figure 7.5.11 compares the percentage of protective orders for which service attempts were made within the statutory requirement of 24 hours, including all domestic violence injunctions for protection.

Fleet Management Turnaround Time

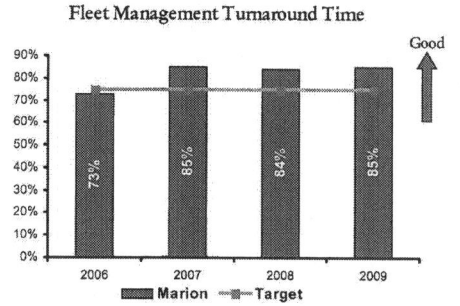

Figure 7.5.13 indicates the percentage of vehicles that were at Fleet Management for 2 days or less. Fleet Management's goal is to have 75 percent of the vehicles back on the road within two days.

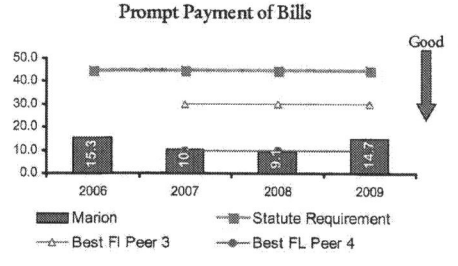

Prompt Payment of Bills

Figure 7.5.15 compares the average number of days before a bill was paid. This time has intentionally increased to capitalize on the additional interest earned during that time period.

Number of Escapes From Court Proceedings

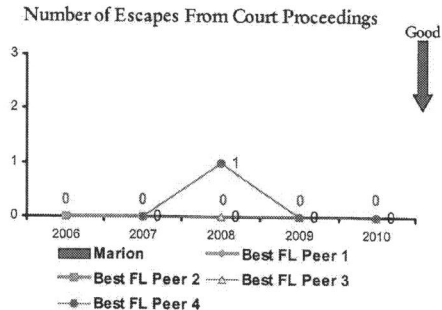

Figure 7.5.12. The Bailiff Division maintains custody and control of approximately 13,000 inmates annually, who are transported from the jail for court appearances. Since 1988, there have been no escapes from the Marion County Judicial Center. This compares favorably to our Best Florida Peers.

Vacancy Rating

Figure 7.5.14 compares the percentage of position vacancies.

Percentage of Domain Uptime

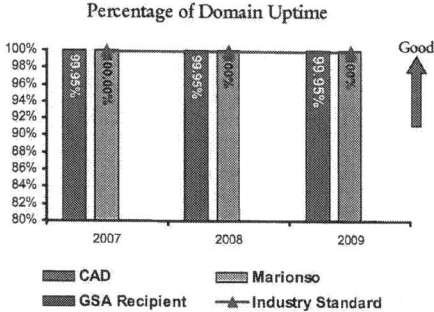

Figure 7.5.16 compares the total uptime percentage for the CAD and Marionso domain. The industry standard is 99.9%

APPENDIX B   159

7.6 Leadership and Social Responsibility Outcomes

We practice Servant Leadership within our organization. Each line level person has the ability and responsibility to identify what is needed to complete their assigned duties for the betterment of the organization and community. Each supervisor is responsible for ensuring that those needs are met, whenever possible and practical, for efficient and productive results.

Strategic Planning Action Step Completion

Figure 7.6.1 shows strategic planning action step completion.

Core Values of Senior Leaders

Figure 7.6.3. Senior leaders are required to lead by personal example and set the agency's directions, mission, core values and expectations that balance the needs of all employees and serve as role models for ethical behavior. This is accomplished through monthly core value videos, human diversity and ethical behavior training. The majority of the employees are satisfied with the core values of the senior leaders, which compares favorably to the Federal Human Capital Survey results of a similar question regarding leaders honesty and integrity.

Figure 7.6.5
The Sheriff of Marion County Florida is a constitutional officer having exclusive powers and authority while serving as the Chief Law Enforcement officer of the county. The Sheriff is elected by the citizens/stakeholders under the same cycle as President of the United States in the general election, which is every four years. The Sheriff is responsible and accountable for the safety of over 300,000 citizens/stakeholders. The current Sheriff, Ed Dean, was first appointed in November 1998 by the late Florida Governor Lawton Chiles and was elected on November 7th 2000 and re-elected in November 2004 and November 2008. The next general election will be in November 2012.

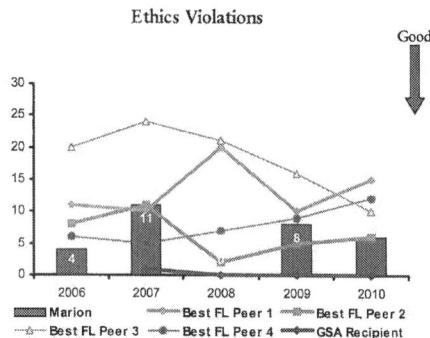

Ethics Violations

Figure 7.6.2. The Florida Department of Law Enforcement is responsible for tracking all sworn law enforcement/corrections officer ethical violations. Agencies that terminate sworn employees for defined Moral Character & agency policy violations or that resign/retire while under investigation are required to be reported to FDLE's Criminal Justice Professionalism Program.

Figure 7.6.4
Marion County Sheriff's Office has not received any audit findings from the external auditor for more than 8 years, which confirms that the Sheriff's Office's internal control structure produces financial statements that are *"free of material misstatement, whether caused by error, fraudulent financial reporting or misappropriation of assets ... An audit also includes assessing the accounting principles used and significant estimates made by management, as well as evaluating the overall financial statement presentation"*. Audit results disclosed no instances of noncompliance that are required to be reported under Government Auditing Standards.

Substantiated EEOC Complaints

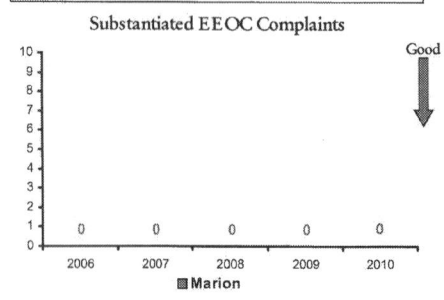

Figure 7.6.6. No Equal Employment Opportunity Commission (EEOC) complaints have been substantiated against the Marion County Sheriff's Office over the past five years.

Compliance with FDLE Training Requirements

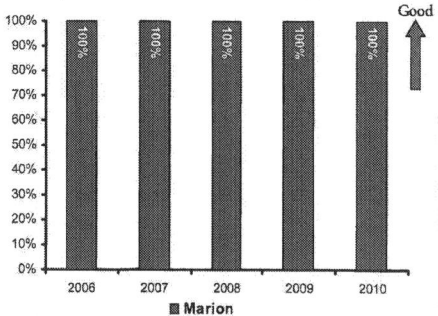

Year	Compliance
2006	100%
2007	100%
2008	100%
2009	100%
2010	100%

■ Marion

Figure 7.6.7 shows compliance with FDLE training requirements for sworn employees.

Accreditation Compliance

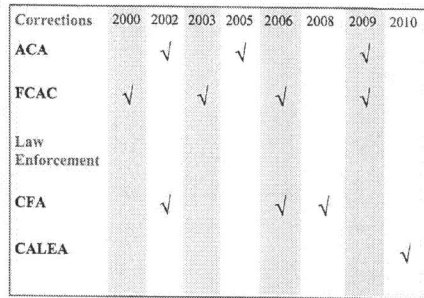

Corrections	2000	2002	2003	2005	2006	2008	2009	2010
ACA			√	√			√	
FCAC	√		√		√		√	
Law Enforcement								
CFA			√			√	√	
CALEA								√

Figure 7.6.8. The Marion County Sheriff's Office has been continuously accredited since 1990. Each process requires an audit to be conducted by the accrediting agency every three (3) years. MCSO has been state accredited by CFA and FCAC since their inception in 1996 (CFA) and 1999 (FCAC).

Florida Model Jail Standards

	2006 Inspection	2007 Inspection	2008 Inspection	2009 Inspection	2010 Inspection
Applicable Standards	268	268	268	268	268
MCSO (# of violations)	2	0	0	0	0
BFP 1	N/A	7	0	0	0
BFP 2	3	N/A	0	0	0
BFP 3	19	5	0	0	0
BFP 4	4	7	0	0	0

Figure 7.6.9 All jails in Florida are required to be inspected on an annual basis. Any noted violation requires the agency to compile a corrective action report demonstrating how the corrections have been made.

Contributions to The United Way

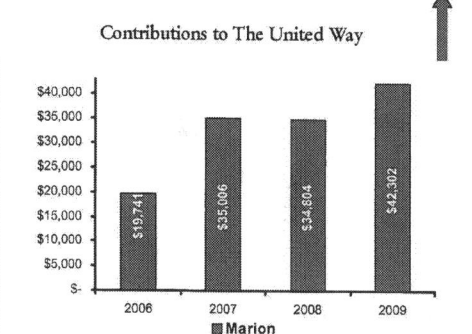

2006	$19,741
2007	$35,006
2008	$34,804
2009	$42,302

■ Marion

Figure 7.6.10. Marion County Sheriff's Office employees and MCSO fundraisers have increased United Way contributions by 114% since 2006.

APPENDIX B 161

Glossary

Glossary of Terms and Abbreviations

ACA	American Correctional Association
AOMC	Administrative Officers Management Course
AOMP	Administrative Officers Management Program
BPD	Belleview Police Department
CAC	Commission on Accreditation for Corrections
CAD	Computer Aided Dispatch
CERT	Certified Emergency Response Team (Jail)
CFA	Commission for Florida Law Enforcement Accreditation
CJSTC	Criminal Justice Standards and Training Commission
CIS	Crisis Intervention Specialist
COPPS	Community Oriented Policing and Problem Solving Services (System); can also refer to
COPS	Citizens Observer Patrol
CTO	Corrections Training Officer
CPA	Certified Public Accountant
DARE	Drug Awareness Resistance Education
DCF	Department of Children and Families
DJJ	Department of Juvenile Justice
DPD	Dunnellon Police Department
DNA	Deoxyribonucleic Acid
EEOC	Equal Employment Opportunity Commission
EMSA	Emergency Medical Services Alliance
EOC	Emergency Operations Center
EPA	Environmental Protection Agency
FACTS	Factual Analysis Criminal Threat Solution
FAQ's	Frequently Asked Questions
FBI	Federal Bureau of Investigation
FBINA	Federal Bureau of Investigation's National Academy
FCAC	Florida Corrections Accreditation Commission
FDLE	Florida Department of Law Enforcement
FTE	Full Time Equivalent/Employee
FTO	Field Training Officer (Law Enforcement)
F.S.S.	Florida State Statute
GED	General Equivalency Diploma
HIDTA	High Intensity Drug Trafficking Area
IT	Information Technology
JAC	Juvenile Assessment Center
K9	Canine
LinX	Law Enforcement Information Exchange
MADET	Multi-Agency Drug Enforcement Team
MCC	Mobile Command Center
MCCAC	Marion County Children's Advocacy Center
MCSO	Marion County Sheriff's Office
MCSO-DEM	Marion County Sheriff's Office Division of Emergency Management
MDT	Mobile Data Terminal
MSTU	Municipal Service Taxing Unit
MYICU	Marion Youth Internet Crimes Unit
NIMS	National Incident Management System
OCC	Ocala Community Care
O.D.	Operational Directive
OPD	Ocala Police Department
PDA	Personal digital assistant
PDCA	Plan-Do-Check-Act
PHS	Prison Health Services
QRT	Quality Review Teams
RDSTF	Regional Domestic Security Task Force

Glossary of Terms and Abbreviations

RPI	Rapid Process Improvement Session-Six Sigma
SARA	Seniors at Risk Assistance Program
SAO	State Attorney's Office
SIR	Supervisor's Incident Report
SOPU	Sexual Offender/Predator Unit
SPI	Southern Police Institute
STAR	Sheriff's Telephone Automated Reporting
STAT	Statistics
SWAT	Special Weapons and Tactics
SWOT	Strengths, Weaknesses, Opportunities, and Threats
UCR	Uniform Crime Reporting
UDEST	Unified Drug Enforcement Strike Team
UPS	Uninterruptible Power Supply
UTT	Uniform Traffic Ticket
WILA	Work in Lieu of Arrest Program
Asp	Expandable defense baton.
Calls for Service	All 9-1-1 emergency and non-emergency calls received by the Marion County Sheriff's Office Communications Center.
Best Florida Peer	Those whom have equal standings with us as in responsibility, size and populations surpassing all others in excellence, achievement or quality.
Decentralization	12 districts, operating from 9 offices, strategically placed throughout the county.
Drug Track	Automated accountability system which allows drug tips to be assigned and evaluated for additional investigation into narcotics crimes.
First Responder	First person on the scene of accident, etc.
Green Team	Complaint tracking program
Listening posts	Any area and/or person from which information is gathered.
Mutual aid:	Cooperative agreements with other law enforcement or governmental agencies
Part 1 Crimes	Crimes identified and measured under the Uniform Crime Reporting System. They include (in order of severity): murder, robbery, sex battery, aggravated battery, burglary, auto theft, and theft.
Pin Maps	Provides a visual depiction of where crime has occurred.
Property Tax Reform:	Proposed property tax reduction.
Self-initiated activity:	Includes traffic stops, neighborhood security checks, suspicious activity, field interviews, etc.
Taser:	Non-lethal weapon that transmits electrical pulses, usually via retractable wires, to contract muscle tissue in order to incapacitate somebody
Tip sheet:	Anonymous complaints received and formatted in writing for investigators to pursue

APPENDIX C

LIBRARY OF SUGGESTED READING

THE PEOPLE CORNERSTONE: SERVANT LEADERSHIP

1. *The Art of Servant Leadership: Designing Your Organization for the Sake of Others*, Tony Baron
2. *Leaders*, Warren Bennis and Burt Nanus
3. *Servant Leader*, Kent Blanchard
4. *The Heart of a Leader: Insights on the Art of Influence*, Kent Blanchard
5. *Lead Like Jesus: Lessons from the Greatest Leadership Role Model of All Time*, Kent Blanchard and Phil Hodges
6. *Good to Great*, Jim Collins
7. *Built to Last*, Jim Collins and Jerry Porras
8. *The 7 Habits of Highly Effective People*, Stephen R. Covey
9. *Principle-Centered Leadership*, Stephen R. Covey
10. *The Eighth Habit: From Effectiveness to Greatness*, Stephen R. Covey
11. *Robert K. Greenleaf: A Life of Servant Leadership*, Don Frick, Larry Spears, and Peter Senge
12. *The Power of Servant Leadership*, Robert Greenleaf, Larry Spears and Peter Vaill
13. *Developing the Leader Within You*, John Maxwell
14. *Winning with People*, John Maxwell
15. *Lincoln on Leadership*, Donald T. Phillips

THE PRINCIPLES CORNERSTONE: CORE VALUES

1. *Jesus' Core Values*. Dan M. Darling
2. *Powered by Principle: Using Core Values to Build World-Class Organizations*. Amie J. Devero

3. *Playing for Keeps: How the World's Most Aggressive and Admired Companies Use Core Values to Manage, Energize and Organize their People, and Promote, Advance, and Achieve their Corporate Missions.* Frederick G. Harmon
4. *The Value of Core Values: Five Keys to Success through Values-Centered Leadership.* Lisa Hutteman
5. *The Entrusted Leader: Develop Rock Solid Core Values.* L. Hollis Jones
6. *Values-Driven Leadership: Discovering and Developing your Core Values for Ministry.* Aubrey Malphurs
7. *Corps Values.* Zell Miller

THE PRIORITIES CORNERSTONE

1. *10 Steps to Successful Strategic Planning.* Susan Barksdale and Terri Lund
2. *Strategic Planning for Public and Non-Profit Organizations.* John M. Bryson
3. *Team-Based Strategic Planning: A Complete Guide to Structuring, Facilitating and Implementing the Process.* C. Davis Fogg
4. *The New Strategic Thinking.* Michael Robert
5. *Organizational Vision, Values, and Mission: Building the Organization of Tomorrow.* Cynthia Scott

THE PERFORMANCE CORNERSTONE

1. *Performance Management.* Robert Bacal
2. *Performance Management: Changing Behavior that Drives Organizational Effectiveness.* Aubrey C. Daniels

3. *Performance Dashboards: Measuring, Monitoring and Managing Your Business.* Wayne W. Eckerson
4. *Quality and Performance Excellence: Management, Organization, and Strategy.* James R. Evans
5. *Harvard Business Essentials: Performance Management; Measure and Improve Effectiveness of your Employees.* Richard Leucke
6. *The Five Key Principles of Corporate Performance Management.* Bob Paladino
7. *Balanced Score Cards and Operational Dashboards with Microsoft Excel.* Ron Person
8. *Performance Management; A New Approach for Driving Business Results.* Elaine Diane Pulakos

APPENDIX D

SERVANT LEADERSHIP: ACCEPTING AND MAINTAINING THE CALL OF SERVICE

By Jenette Nagy and Edited by Bill Berkowitz and Jerry Schultz
(Community Tool Box: http://ctb.ku.edu/
Reprinted with permission)

Servant Leadership: Accepting and Maintaining the Call of Service

Contributed by Jenette Nagy

Main Section

Edited by
Bill
Berkowitz
and Jerry
Schultz

What are the qualities of the servant leader?

How do you become a servant leader?
How do you find inspiration?

Note: The idea of servant leadership comes from the pioneering work of Robert K. Greenleaf.

Let's face it, leadership has a bad rap. From sex scandals to embezzlement, from the power hungry monster to the inept bureaucrat, many people have a difficult time putting faith in their leaders, and working with them efficiently to reach shared goals.

And yet, there are people leading for what we might call the "right" reasons; people who use leadership as a means to help others, instead of as a way to gain personal power. These people come to leadership because they want to be to serve others better.

How is that? In their service, they have found that they can do the most good by accepting the responsibilities and possibilities of leadership. We call these people who become leaders out of a desire to serve more effectively *servant leaders*.

In the next few pages, we will explore some of the ideas of servant leadership. Next, we'll look briefly at how someone becomes a servant leader. Finally, we'll discuss an equally important topic - how the servant leader can maintain his or her desire to serve over the long run.

What are the qualities of the servant leader?

Many of the other sections in this chapter of the Tool Box have discussed different qualities of leadership, such as influencing others, decision-making, and identifying needs. All of these qualities are true of servant leaders as well. But the term servant leader asks for something more; a different mindset, perhaps. It is truly a unique take on the idea of leadership.

What follows is a list of some of the most important qualities of servant leadership. Some of the following ideas and actions are unique to servant leadership. Others, while they may be found in all types of leadership, are simply emphasized more strongly by servant leaders.

The servant leader believes himself "first among equals." This idea is at the very core of servant leadership. A servant leader does not consider himself *above* those he leads. Rather, he is *primus inter pares* from Latin, meaning "first among equals." That is, he sees those he leads as peers to teach and to learn from. He is willing to lead others in order to reach an agreed upon goal, but he doesn't believe that being the leader makes him better than others.

Because of this, the servant leader is a consummate team builder. She will draw on the strengths of followers, and be a follower *herself* when appropriate. Such a leader doesn't lead by decree or dictate. Instead, he or she leads by allowing everyone to do what they do well. In this sense, she might be like the ringmaster at the circus - directing people to their proper position, then stepping out of the spotlight and letting them shine.

This idea is hardly new - in fact, it was captured several thousand years ago in the following verses adapted from the *Tao Te Ching*:

The reason why rivers and seas receive the homage of a hundred mountain streams is that they keep below them. Thus they are able to reign over all the mountain streams. So the sage, wishing to be above others, stays below them; wishing to be before them, the sage stays behind them. Thus, though the sage be above others, they do not feel the weight; though the sage be before others, they do not count it as an injury.

Like the sage, the servant leader's style of leadership might well be called *unassuming*. And this style of guidance - where people, as equals, are able to voice their concerns and work to their potential - is not a heavy weight on followers. Instead, the servant leader shares burdens and benefits equally with these peers. Everyone involved benefits.

The servant leader uses power honestly. A servant leader uses leadership and power legitimately, for the good of the people he or she serves. She sees leadership as a *means* to obtain the general good, not as a desired personal *end*.

For those of us watching people in power, the difference is very clear. We don't look up to the loan shark who uses his muscle and brags of his brawn, nor to the politician who uses slick talk and brags of his skill. We look up to the Mother Theresa's of the world; the Nelson Mandela's They are servant leaders who have filled their positions with integrity.

Robert Greenleaf, in his essay *The Servant as Leader*, puts it this way: "It begins with the natural feeling that one wants to serve, to serve first. Then conscious choice brings one to aspire to lead. The difference manifests itself in the care taken by the servant - first to make sure that other people's highest priority needs are being served."

Do our leaders always succeed in this arena? Hardly. They may fall from this - and we, as servant leaders, may fall from it as well. We're human. Nonetheless, it is an ideal we look up to in our public institutions and in our leaders. And by continuing to try, we may inspire our followers to a life of service as well.

The servant leader understands the importance of day-to-day details. When we think of great leadership, many of us think about what may be termed, "The Great Talk." We think about Martin Luther King's dream; we think about what we can do for our country. We think about fire and brimstone, or slogans from revolutionaries.

And yet, the truth of the matter is these speeches make up a very small portion leadership, and their need is even smaller for a servant leader. Being a servant leader is more about the one-on-one discussions and in taking care of the everyday details.

Exercise:

Think about a group of people you have worked with or witnessed that was particularly effective. Things got done and done *well,* and members truly seemed to enjoy their work. Who was the leader, officially or unofficially? What did (s)he do? What was his or her style of management?

The servant leader listens to and cares for his or her constituents. Servant leaders are willing to take the time to listen to what others have to say. In fact, they are more than willing - they actively seek out the opinions and ideas of these followers. This is of top importance to the servant leader.

And from this listening, a relationship of mutual respect can grow. Listening is innate to the servant leader - caring about others is a part of who they are. They can use that skill and learn from their followers; they aren't only teachers.

For ways to become a better listener, check out an active listening exercise in our Tools section.

The servant leader helps people get what they want. The servant leader cares about people; and so she will naturally find out what they want, and help them to get it.

Sometimes, however, a servant leader seems to want something very different than her constituents. What happens then?

Often the greater goal may be the same, but people will have different ideas in mind of how to get it. For example, a servant leader may want to meet diplomatically with leaders of the opposition in a case of environmental pollution, while others in the group want to confront them.

When faced with this type of situation, a servant leader tries to phrase things in the proper terms, or put them in the right light to make people see things his way. You catch more flies with honey than with vinegar, goes the old adage; an effective leader explains and discusses things in a manner so that common goals are clear, or the advantages of doing things a certain way become obvious.

Wait a minute, you might say. This is all starting to sound a little bit negative - all of this talk of selling things, and putting them in the right light. Does a good leader, then, essentially dupe his or her followers?

Not at all. Remember, we said at the beginning that the servant leader must lead honestly, for the right reason(s). But if you speak English, and want to hold a discussion with someone from Brazil, you would have to change the way you speak to him or her. You would need to learn Portuguese. Then, you could go ahead and have a good talk.

While most cases aren't that extreme, the message is clear: a servant leader knows - and uses - the language of his constituents. Take the following example:

The leader of a teen pregnancy prevention program wanted the support of the local Catholic priest. However, he knew he probably wouldn't get very far by discussing the program's "condom sense" campaign. Instead, he and the priest talked about their common work. They both promote abstinence, and both of them have a strong desire that young people's lives are as full and healthy as possible. In leaving the discussion, they agreed to work on several projects together, and the priest agreed not to loudly oppose other work by the group that he did not agree with. In the end, a great alliance was formed.

The lesson? *Start where people are.*

Before we go on, it's important to note here that the servant leader is not closed minded. He will do his best to convince others to see things his way; that much is true. However, as we have said, the servant leader listens and learns from his constituents. He is open to improvement. So, if he is convinced that the other is right, he will gracefully accede to the other's suggestion.

The servant leader stretches his or her constituents. While, as we saw in the last point that the servant leader starts where people are, he doesn't *stop* there. Instead, the servant leader helps others see the potential that exists. This can be personally (I know you can finish a marathon), as well as in the community (can you just imagine what this neighborhood would look like with fresh paint and some trees?). A servant leader helps people to do things they didn't know they could. She sits down with her constituents to set goals that are both feasible and challenging.

The servant leader inspires others to service. Finally, a servant leader knows she can't do it all alone - and frankly, she wouldn't want to if she could. A servant leader wants to work with and *for* others. To do so, then, the leader must be able to inspire those she serves to serve others.

How does the servant leader inspire people? The methods he uses to inspire people to serve aren't necessarily any different from methods used by *any* leader to inspire others to do anything - or really, by *anyone* who inspires people. The desire of a servant leader to help others may be inspirational in itself, but people may be inspired by many, many different things.

We might answer this question, then, by looking briefly at inspiration in general. We can start on a personal level. What causes us to jump out of our seat when a speaker is talking; that convinces us to send money to a child we'll never meet? What is this fountain of inspiration? What do we need to do?

Exercise:

Before you go on, write down a list of five leaders you either know personally or know about – five people whom you admire tremendously. Why do they grab you as they do? What do they do? How do they do it? What do you like about them? Do they all have the same style of leadership? If not, how do they differ?

Chances are the five people whose names you have in front of you are very different. One might be quiet, another brash. One might yell, another question. One might love publicity, another have a healthy distaste for (or distrust of) the media. Perhaps you have someone on the list that you have never even seen, but something he wrote sent chills of excitement running down your spine.

In any case, the folks you have in front of you are probably quite different. That's true among leaders in general, and even among servant leaders. If you look closely, however, some qualities might occur again and again. A partial list of qualities that inspire include:

- Honesty
- Awareness
- Empathy
- Passion
- Ability to overcome obstacles, especially obstacles that followers have grappled with
- A sense of joyfulness

A servant leader adapts to fit the situation. If your house is on fire, you don't want the firefighter to say, "Now what do you think would be the most optimal use of time and direction at the present moment?" Rather, you probably want to hear, "The ladder is right there, and we're going to get you and the kids out of here."

On the other hand, if you are at work discussing a major change in your organization, "What do you think we should do?" becomes an appropriate question. In fact, you might become pretty angry if you aren't asked.

To inspire, then, a servant leader gauges each situation and responds to each individually. When appropriate, she will pass over the reins to someone whose leadership style is more appropriate to the situation - she works with people's strengths. A good leader understands when she is not necessarily the best person for the job; she knows her strengths as well as her weaknesses, and can gracefully pass on opportunities best suited to other individuals.

How do you become a servant leader?

As you can see, becoming a servant leader is more a state of mind than a set of directions. So unlike many of the other sections in the Tool Box, becoming a servant leader does not follow a step by step process. (First, you become honest. Second, you care about people...). However, there are things that the servant leader does, rather than simply believes. You can work on these skills to keep the *servant* part of *servant leader* fresh in your mind. Many of these are discussed in detail in other sections, and so we will simply mention them here. They include:

- Listening to others
- Involving others

- Promoting teamwork rather than individual decision making
- Enhance problem-solving skills

These topics are discussed in some depth in **Chapter 16:** *Group Facilitation and Problem-Solving.* Also, see Tools at the end of this section for activities to promote communication and team building.

How do you find inspiration?

The servant leader, as we have discussed, is someone who wants to help others first - and thus, by definition, take care of himself second. However, maybe that is sometimes a problem. Perhaps, as a leader, you feel you are losing your edge. You want to help people - or at least you used to. But you're wearing down. You're getting tired. The problem you took on seems larger than ever, and the only thing larger is the pile on your desk. You don't remember the last time you saw your spouse. You want to hand over the reins. You don't want to serve, you want to be spoiled for a while. You want to run off to Jamaica, and not ever, ever return.

Sound familiar? And if so, what can be done about it? What inspires - or reinspires - the servant leader? Where do we get the energy, the excitement, and the persistence to enthrall others and lead them to be active champions of our cause? What moves us to move others?

For the leader on the road to burn out - or for someone who wants to stay away from that path altogether - it's not always easy to remain inspired, and full of excitement about the cause. And yet, *it may be the most important thing you can do.* Burning out and giving up is all too real a possibility. Think of it this way - if you allow yourself to burn out, a light has gone, robbing your cause of a powerful weapon.

A good leader, then - a strong, in-it-for-the-long-run leader - takes care of him or herself *along with helping others*. It's easy for many of us to get caught up in our work, and not consider our own needs. Or, if we do take care of ourselves, we do so haphazardly, when levels of frustration are high and the floodgates finally burst.

To avoid that, then, the servant leader thinks about his or her needs on a continuous basis. He takes care of himself before disaster strikes. To avoid that, then, the servant leader thinks about his or her needs on a continuous basis. He takes care of himself before disaster strikes.

This sounds contradictory, you might say; I just read that the servant leader serves first. True. But a leader must get something out of her work, and she must acknowledge that gain, or the path to giving up becomes very short. Both elements must be there. Think about two overlapping circles:

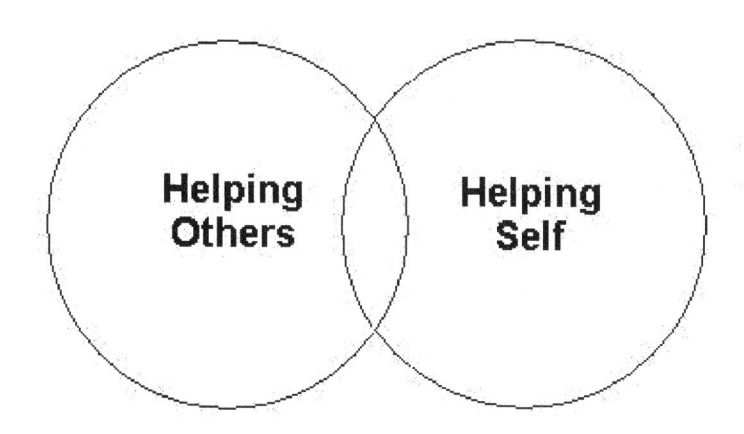

Helping Others   **Helping Self**

One of these circles represents the servant leader's desire to help others; the other represents her need to help herself. Ideally, a servant leader should find herself doing both of these things, in a place where these circles overlap.

So what are some things that the leader can do to remain inspired and excited about his or her work? Answers are as individual as every leader is. However, consider these possibilities, which have worked for many leaders. Might any of them work for you?

- *Take time for you.* You may think you don't have time for a vacation, or for an afternoon off: but can you really afford not to? You need time to regroup, and to replenish your well. There are many ways you can do this. It could be in daily meditation or on a jog, or by taking a day to do something you love. It could be almost anything: going to a play or enjoying a picnic; taking a pottery class or watching a football game. Whatever you do, it should be something *just for you* that you will enjoy and find renewing. And it should have nothing to do with work.
- *Read* - and not simply news and your work. Read novels, biographies, or anything else you enjoy. One constant among many of our historical leaders is how much they read. Reading inspires creativity and helps you to see the "big picture" more clearly. By doing so, you make associations you wouldn't have otherwise. In short, it helps you keep all of life in your consciousness.
- *Have others to sustain you.* We've all heard the phrase, "It's lonely at the top." That can be true for servant leaders, too. In fact, when you get right down to it, it can be lonely wherever you are in the pile. All of us need people who can help us and who support us in our challenges and our joys.

For servant leaders, it is important that we choose these people well. That's because unfortunately, if we don't consciously choose these people, we often hoist our needs on the wrong people.

We might get a lot of this support from people in our personal lives: spouses, family members, and friends. Sometimes, however, it's helpful to get support from people within your field, who have dealt with some of the same challenges and excitements as you have. Two ways to have such relationships are:

- Having a mentor. We are always learning; hopefully, our education never ends. By standing on the shoulders of those who came before us, our view is much broader. Thus, maintaining a mentoring relationship can be an excellent way you to help you continue growing professionally.
- Developing strong peer relationships. Talking with other leaders, especially in your field, can be very helpful. This is one way in which professional meetings and conferences can be useful. By speaking to other leaders, you start understanding that other people have the exact same problems you are dealing with. It can help you realize you are not alone.

Exercise:

Think of someone whose leadership you admire or who you admire professionally in other ways. Preferably, choose someone who has been working in their field for many years. Ask them where they receive *their* support. When they are frustrated, who do they turn to? Are there similar possibilities or people in our own life? Would the same forms of support work for you?

- *Challenge yourself.* When the "old routine" doesn't work for you any longer, find new mountains to climb. Challenge yourself with new directions and possibilities. This could be by starting a new program, forming a new collaboration, or revamping an existing project. Anything that will get your excitement flowing again can work; the possibilities are boundless.

- *Look at the whole picture.* That is to say, remember the whole forest, and don't let yourself get hung up in the trees. Sometimes, we can get hung up in the daily frustrations of our work. That's when it's time to remind ourselves of our broader vision, whether it is an end to child abuse, a thriving neighborhood, or a world without prejudice. In doing so, we may be more willing to see these frustrations as small obstacles we are willing to hurdle, instead of impossible mountains that aren't worth our efforts.
- *Celebrate the small wins.* World peace, for example, is a lofty goal. It's not one you or even your organization will achieve alone. In fact, it may never be completely achieved, but many of us feel it's still worth striving for. So when you do accomplish a piece of that peace, celebrate your accomplishment. For suggestions, see **Chapter 41, Section 1:** *Arranging Celebrations.*

In Summary:

The servant leader sees leadership much in the same way a carpenter sees a hammer. A hammer is a tool - and a very important tool at that. It can be used build; to create; to realize a dream. And with one wrong hit, a very painful thumb.

Leadership, too, allows one to develop dreams. It opens doors and allows opportunities to be realized. However, it's something to be careful with. For like the hammer, mistakes can be costly. Worse yet, leadership, like that hammer, can be used to destroy instead of create; to hurt people instead of help them. And without paying proper attention to ourselves, it can destroy the leader as well.

The wise servant, then, is as careful with this power as she would be with that hammer, always trying to make sure to hit the nail on the head.

Community Tool Box: <u>http://ctb.ku.edu/</u>
(Used by Permission)

Resources

Print

Greenleaf, R. K. (1976). <u>Servant leadership: A journey into the nature of legitimate power and greatness.</u> New York, NY: Paulist Press.

Covey, S. (1992). <u>Principle-centered leadership</u>. New York, NY: Simon and Schuster.

Internet

Greenleaf Center for Servant Leadership provides resources for understanding the principles and practices of servant leadership.

The Heartland Center for Leadership Development

ABOUT THE AUTHOR

Ed Dean served for fourteen years as the elected Sheriff of Marion County, Florida. Mr. Dean was appointed as Sheriff in 1998 by the late Governor Lawton Chiles. He was then successfully elected as Sheriff in 2000, 2004, 2008 and served until January, 2013. The Marion County Sheriff's office received the coveted Florida Governor's Sterling Award in 2008 for Performance Excellence and was recognized again in 2011 for Sustained Excellence.

Ed Dean earned a B. A. degree from Michigan State University (with honors) in 1967 and a Juris Doctor degree from the University of Florida College of Law (with honors) in 1970. He also graduated from the F.B.I. Law Enforcement Executive Program at the F.B.I. Academy in 2000, from the Florida Department of Law Enforcement Executive Program in 2001, and received an Honorary Doctorate of Humane Letters from St. Leo University in 2009. Mr. Dean completed Harvard University John F. Kennedy School of Government's program, "Driving Government Performance: Leadership Strategies that Produce Results" in 2012.

Mr. Dean is active in community affairs and has previous experience in law and in forming, leading and managing private and public sector enterprises. Earlier in his career, he served as an Adjunct Professor at the University of Florida College of Law.

Ed Dean is the author of four other books, including *Luctor et Emergo* (ISBN-10:1452855844) and *Angel in Disguise*, (ISBN-13:978-1460904602), which are biographies of his deaf parents and their amazing story of the challenges they faced in life and how they overcame them. He is also the co-author of *Inspiration for Fifty Years* (ISBN-13:978-1494234980), which is a history of Townley Engineering and Manufacturing Co., Inc. and the story of overcoming hardship through the faith of founders, J. O. "Jake" and Helen Townley. *Servant Governing* is a companion book to *The Servant Organization*, ISBN-13:978-1492988106, also by Mr. Dean. Each of these books is available through both www.Amazon.com and www.Kindle.Amazon.com.